a year of
AFGHANS

LEISURE ARTS, INC.
and
OXMOOR HOUSE, INC.

EDITORIAL STAFF

Vice President and Editor-in-Chief: Anne Van Wagner Childs
Executive Director: Sandra Graham Case
Editorial Director: Susan Frantz Wiles
Publications Director: Carla Bentley
Creative Art Director: Gloria Bearden
Senior Graphics Art Director: Melinda Stout

PRODUCTION
Managing Editor: Susan White Sullivan
Senior Technical Editor: Cathy Hardy
Instructional Editors: Sarah J. Green, Tammy Kreimeyer,
  and Lois Phillips

EDITORIAL
Managing Editor: Linda L. Trimble
Coordinating Editor: Terri Leming Davidson
Associate Editor: Darla Burdette Kelsay
Assistant Editors: Stacey Robertson Marshall
  and Janice Teipen Wojcik

ART
Graphics Art Director: Rhonda Hodge Shelby
Senior Graphics Illustrator: Sonya McFatrich
Graphics Illustrators: Mary Ellen Wilhelm, Dana Vaughn,
  Roberta Aulwes, and Keith Melton

BUSINESS STAFF

Publisher: Bruce Akin
Vice President and General Manager:
  Thomas L. Carlisle
Retail Sales Director: Richard Tignor
Vice President, Retail Marketing: Pam Stebbins
Retail Marketing Director: Margaret Sweetin
Retail Customer Service Manager: Carolyn Pruss
General Merchandise Manager: Cathy Laird
Vice President, Finance: Tom Siebenmorgen
Distribution Director: Rob Theime

A Year of Afghans
Published by Leisure Arts, Inc., and Oxmoor House, Inc.

ISSN 1096-5505
Hardcover ISBN 1-57486-116-6
Softcover ISBN 1-57486-117-4

As you journey through A Year of Afghans, *you'll rediscover the simple pleasures of crocheted wraps. Think about how much you really love the warmth and comfort that handmade afghans bring to your life, and how much they enhance your surroundings. You might also find that what you most enjoy is the creative process — the quiet moments spent making something that's uniquely yours.*

Here are 52 beautiful throws from which to choose. Our radiant color photographs show each afghan in complete detail, so you can see for yourself how the colors and patterns combine to create a masterpiece. Since many of us are pressed for time, we've also included afghans that work up quickly for each season.

You'll uncover a cozy collection of comforts in toasty hues for the cold winter months, plus some snuggly blankets for baby. The fresh days of springtime unearth a bounty of throws with garden blooms, and summer sails into your home with shades and patterns that reflect the leisurely weeks we love best. Autumn ushers in a spectacular collection ablaze with vibrant color.

Enjoy sharing your passion for crochet with family and friends — for a lasting gift of warmth, there's nothing like a handmade afghan!

table of contents

BUFFALO CHECK

Black and teal make a striking team for this buffalo check wrap. The dramatic throw works up quickly holding two strands of yarn together.

January

Finished Size: 46¹/₂" x 65¹/₂"

MATERIALS
   Worsted Weight Yarn:
      Black - 35 ounces,
         (990 grams, 2,200 yards)
      Teal - 35 ounces,
         (990 grams, 2,200 yards)
   Crochet hook, size N (9.00 mm) **or** size
     needed for gauge

GAUGE: In pattern, 9 sts and 8 rows = 4"

Gauge Swatch: 4" x 4"
Ch 11 **loosely**.
Work same as Afghan for 8 rows.

Note: Each row is worked across length of Afghan holding two strands of yarn together. When joining yarn and finishing off, always leave a 9" end to be worked into fringe.

With Black, ch 149 **loosely**.
Row 1 (Right side)**:** Dc in fourth ch from hook and in next ch, (ch 3, skip next 3 chs, dc in next 3 chs) across: 24 ch-3 sps.
Note: Loop a short piece of yarn around any stitch to mark Row 1 as **right** side.
Row 2: Ch 3, turn; skip first 3 dc, working over next ch-3 and in skipped chs of beginning ch, dc in next 3 chs, ch 3, ★ skip next 3 dc, working over next ch-3 and in skipped chs of beginning ch, dc in next 3 chs, ch 3; repeat from ★ across to last 3 sts, skip next 2 dc, slip st in last st; finish off: 25 ch-3 sps.
Row 3: With **right** side facing and working over slip st, join Teal with slip st in first st one row **below**; ch 3, working over next ch-3, dc in next 2 dc one row **below**, ★ ch 3, skip next 3 dc, working over next ch-3, dc in next 3 dc one row **below**; repeat from ★ across: 24 ch-3 sps.
Row 4: Ch 3, turn; skip first 3 dc, working over next ch-3, dc in next 3 dc one row **below**, ch 3, ★ skip next 3 dc, working over next ch-3, dc in next 3 dc one row **below**, ch 3; repeat from ★ across to last 3 sts, skip next 2 dc, slip st in last st; finish off: 25 ch-3 sps.
Row 5: With **right** side facing and working over slip st, join Black with slip st in first st one row **below**; ch 3, working over next ch-3, dc in next 2 dc one row **below**, ★ ch 3, skip next 3 dc, working over next ch-3, dc in next 3 dc one row **below**; repeat from ★ across: 24 ch-3 sps.
Row 6: Ch 3, turn; skip first 3 dc, working over next ch-3, dc in next 3 dc one row **below**, ch 3, ★ skip next 3 dc, working over next ch-3, dc in next 3 dc one row **below**, ch 3; repeat from ★ across to last 3 sts, skip next 2 dc, slip st in last st; finish off: 25 ch-3 sps.
Repeat Rows 3-6 until Afghan measures approximately 46¹/₂" from beginning ch, ending by working Row 5.
Last Row: Turn; slip st in first 3 dc, ★ working over next ch-3, dc in next 3 dc one row **below**, slip st in next 3 sts; repeat from ★ across; finish off.

Holding 6 strands of corresponding color together, add additional fringe across short edge of Afghan (*Figs. 31b & d, page 143*).
Holding 8 strands of corresponding color together, add fringe to opposite edge of Afghan.

6

DELIGHTFUL MEDLEY

Winter evenings spent wrapped in this afghan, which features a delightful medley of six colors, will be especially cozy. Easy clusters add texture to the pretty stripes, and the long, flowing fringe is partially created each time you change colors.

Finished Size: 50" x 69"

MATERIALS
Worsted Weight Yarn:
  Pink - 13 ounces, (370 grams, 855 yards)
  Green - 13 ounces, (370 grams, 855 yards)
  Ecru - 13 ounces, (370 grams, 855 yards)
  Peach - 13 ounces, (370 grams, 855 yards)
  Tan - 6 ounces, (170 grams, 395 yards)
  Blue - 6 ounces, (170 grams, 395 yards)
  Crochet hook, size I (5.50 mm) **or** size needed
    for gauge

GAUGE: In pattern, 12 sts and 12 rows = 4"

Gauge Swatch: 5"w x 4"h
Ch 16 **loosely**.
Work same as Afghan for 12 rows.

Note: Each row is worked across length of Afghan. When
  joining yarn and finishing off, always leave a 9"
  end to be worked into fringe.

STITCH GUIDE

CLUSTER
Ch 3, ★ YO, insert hook in third ch from hook, YO and pull
up a loop, YO and draw through 2 loops on hook; repeat
from ★ once **more**, YO and draw through all 3 loops on
hook *(Fig. 15a, page 140)*.

COLOR SEQUENCE
One row **each**: Pink, (Green, Tan, Ecru, Peach, Pink) twice,
★ (Green, Blue, Ecru, Peach, Pink) twice, (Green, Tan, Ecru,
Peach, Pink) twice; repeat from ★ throughout.

AFGHAN BODY

With Pink, ch 208 **loosely**.
Row 1 (Right side)**:** Sc in third ch from hook (**2 skipped chs
count as first hdc**), (dc in next ch, sc in next ch) across to
last ch, hdc in last ch; finish off: 207 sts.
Note: Loop a short piece of yarn around any stitch to mark
Row 1 as **right** side.

Row 2: With **wrong** side facing, join next color with sc in first
hdc *(see Joining With Sc, page 142)*; dc in next sc, sc in
next dc, work Cluster, skip next sc, sc in next dc, ★ (dc in next
st, sc in next dc) 3 times, work Cluster, skip next sc, sc in next
dc; repeat from ★ across to last 2 sts, dc in next sc, sc in last
hdc; finish off: 26 Clusters.
Row 3: With **right** side facing, join next color with slip st in
first sc; ch 2 **(counts as first hdc, now and throughout)**, sc
in next dc, dc in next sc, working **behind** next Cluster, dc in
skipped sc one row **below** Cluster, dc in next sc, ★ (sc in next
dc, dc in next sc) 3 times, working **behind** next Cluster, dc in
skipped sc one row **below** Cluster, dc in next sc; repeat from ★
across to last 2 sts, sc in next dc, hdc in last sc; finish off.
Row 4: With **wrong** side facing, join next color with sc in first
hdc; (dc in next st, sc in next dc) 3 times, ★ work Cluster, skip
next sc, sc in next dc, (dc in next st, sc in next st) 3 times;
repeat from ★ across; finish off: 25 Clusters.
Row 5: With **right** side facing, join next color with slip st in
first sc; ch 2, ★ (sc in next dc, dc in next sc) 3 times, working
behind next Cluster, dc in skipped sc one row **below** Cluster,
dc in next sc; repeat from ★ across to last 6 sts, sc in next dc,
(dc in next sc, sc in next dc) twice, hdc in last sc; finish off.
Repeat Rows 2-5 until Afghan measures approximately 50" from
beginning ch, ending by working a **right** side row; finish off.

EDGING
FIRST SIDE
With **right** side facing, working across last row, and using same
color as last row, join yarn with slip st in first st; (ch 1, skip next
st, slip st in next st) across; finish off.

SECOND SIDE
With **right** side facing and working in free loops of beginning ch
(Fig. 26b, page 142), join Pink with slip st in first ch; (ch 1,
skip next ch, slip st in next ch) across; finish off.

Holding 2 strands of corresponding color together, add
additional fringe to each stripe across short edges of Afghan
(Figs. 31b & d, page 143).

CASUAL COMFORT

Rich, toasty hues warm this casual throw. Stripes in varying widths and a simple edging of single crochet give the afghan a sporty look.

Finished Size: 40" x 60½"

MATERIALS
Worsted Weight Yarn:
Tan - 14½ ounces, (410 grams, 910 yards)
Navy - 11 ounces, (310 grams, 690 yards)
Maroon - 6 ounces, (170 grams, 375 yards)
Ecru - 5 ounces, (140 grams, 315 yards)
Crochet hook, size J (6.00 mm) **or** size needed for gauge

GAUGE: In pattern, 13 sts = 4"; 12 rows = 4½"

Gauge Swatch: 4"w x 4½"h
Ch 14 **loosely**.
Work same as Afghan for 12 rows.
Finish off.

Note: Each row is worked across length of Afghan.

AFGHAN BODY

With Tan, ch 196 **loosely**.
Row 1 (Right side)**:** Sc in second ch from hook and in each ch across: 195 sc.
Note: Loop a short piece of yarn around any stitch to mark Row 1 as **right** side.
Row 2: Ch 4 **(counts as first tr, now and throughout)**, turn; tr in same st, ★ skip next sc, (tr, ch 1, tr) in next sc; repeat from ★ across to last 2 sc, skip next sc, 2 tr in last sc: 96 ch-1 sps.
Row 3: Ch 1, turn; sc in first tr, ★ skip next tr, sc in sp **before** next tr *(Fig. 28, page 142)* and in next ch-1 sp; repeat from ★ across to last 3 tr, skip next tr, sc in sp **before** next tr, skip next tr, sc in last tr changing to Ecru *(Fig. 27a, page 142)*: 195 sc.
Row 4: Ch 1, turn; sc in each sc across changing to Maroon in last sc.
Row 5: Ch 3 **(counts as first dc, now and throughout)**, turn; dc in same st, ★ skip next sc, (dc, ch 1, dc) in next sc; repeat from ★ across to last 2 sc, skip next sc, 2 dc in last sc changing to Navy in last dc: 96 ch-1 sps.

Row 6: Ch 1, turn; sc in first dc, (skip next dc, sc in sp **before** next dc and in next ch-1 sp) across to last 3 dc, skip next dc, sc in sp **before** next dc, skip next dc, sc in last dc: 195 sc.
Row 7: Ch 1, turn; sc in each sc across.
Row 8: Ch 3, turn; dc in same st, ★ skip next sc, (dc, ch 1, dc) in next sc; repeat from ★ across to last 2 sc, skip next sc, 2 dc in last sc: 96 ch-1 sps.
Row 9: Ch 1, turn; sc in first dc, (skip next dc, sc in sp **before** next dc and in next ch-1 sp) across to last 3 dc, skip next dc, sc in sp **before** next dc, skip next dc, sc in last dc: 195 sc.
Row 10: Ch 1, turn; sc in each sc across changing to Maroon in last sc.
Row 11: Ch 3, turn; dc in same st, ★ skip next sc, (dc, ch 1, dc) in next sc; repeat from ★ across to last 2 sc, skip next sc, 2 dc in last sc changing to Ecru in last dc: 96 ch-1 sps.
Row 12: Ch 1, turn; sc in first dc, (skip next dc, sc in sp **before** next dc and in next ch-1 sp) across to last 3 dc, skip next dc, sc in sp **before** next dc, skip next dc, sc in last dc changing to Tan: 195 sc.
Row 13: Ch 1, turn; sc in each sc across.
Row 14: Ch 4, turn; tr in same st, ★ skip next sc, (tr, ch 1, tr) in next sc; repeat from ★ across to last 2 sc, skip next sc, 2 tr in last sc: 96 ch-1 sps.
Row 15: Ch 1, turn; sc in first tr, (skip next tr, sc in sp **before** next tr and in next ch-1 sp) across to last 3 tr, skip next tr, sc in sp **before** next tr, skip next tr, sc in last tr changing to Ecru: 195 sc.
Row 16: Ch 1, turn; sc in each sc across changing to Navy in last sc.
Row 17: Ch 3, turn; dc in same st, ★ skip next sc, (dc, ch 1, dc) in next sc; repeat from ★ across to last 2 sc, skip next sc, 2 dc in last sc changing to Ecru in last dc: 96 ch-1 sps.
Row 18: Ch 1, turn; sc in first dc, (skip next dc, sc in sp **before** next dc and in next ch-1 sp) across to last 3 dc, skip next dc, sc in sp **before** next dc, skip next dc, sc in last dc changing to Tan: 195 sc.
Row 19: Ch 1, turn; sc in each sc across.

Row 20: Ch 4, turn; tr in same st, ★ skip next sc, (tr, ch 1, tr) in next sc; repeat from ★ across to last 2 sc, skip next sc, 2 tr in last sc: 96 ch-1 sps.

Row 21: Ch 1, turn; sc in first tr, (skip next tr, sc in sp **before** next tr and in next ch-1 sp) across to last 3 tr, skip next tr, sc in sp **before** next tr, skip next tr, sc in last tr changing to Ecru: 195 sc.

Rows 22-105: Repeat Rows 4-21, 4 times; then repeat Rows 4-15 once **more**; at end of Row 105, do **not** change colors; do **not** finish off.

EDGING
FIRST SIDE

Row 1: Ch 1, do **not** turn; sc evenly across end of rows.
Row 2: Ch 1, turn; sc in each sc across; finish off.

SECOND SIDE

Row 1: With **right** side facing and working in end of rows, join Tan with slip st in first row; ch 1, sc evenly across.
Row 2: Ch 1, turn; sc in each sc across; finish off.

NOSTALGIC RIPPLE

Nothing warms the heart in winter like the comforts of home. This nostalgic throw, which features cascades of clusters, has a lush texture that will tempt you to stay snuggled inside all season long.

Finished Size: 46" x 66"

MATERIALS
Worsted Weight Yarn:
    49 ounces, (1,390 grams, 3,080 yards)
Crochet hook, size H (5.00 mm) **or** size needed
    for gauge

GAUGE: Each repeat from point to point = 5";
        7 rows = 4³/4"

Gauge Swatch: 10"w x 4³/4"h
Ch 56 **loosely**.
Work same as Afghan for 7 rows.
Finish off.

STITCH GUIDE

DECREASE (uses next 2 sts)
★ YO, insert hook in **next** st, YO and pull up a loop, YO and draw through 2 loops on hook; repeat from ★ once **more**, YO and draw through all 3 loops on hook **(counts as one dc)**.

ENDING DECREASE (uses last 3 sts)
YO, insert hook in next st, YO and pull up a loop, YO and draw through 2 loops on hook, YO, skip next st, insert hook in last st, YO and pull up a loop, YO and draw through 2 loops on hook, YO and draw through all 3 loops on hook **(counts as one dc)**.

CLUSTER
Ch 3, YO twice, insert hook in third ch from hook, YO and pull up a loop, (YO and draw through 2 loops on hook) twice, ★ YO twice, insert hook in same ch, YO and pull up a loop, (YO and draw through 2 loops on hook) twice; repeat from ★ 2 times **more**, YO and draw through all 5 loops on hook *(Fig. 15a, page 140)*.

Ch 238 **loosely**.

Row 1 (Right side): Dc in fifth ch from hook and in next 9 chs, place a marker around third skipped ch for Edging placement, ch 1, skip next ch, dc in next ch, ch 3, dc in next ch, ch 1, ★ skip next ch, dc in next 8 chs, decrease, skip next 2 chs, decrease, dc in next 8 chs, ch 1, skip next ch, dc in next ch, ch 3, dc in next ch, ch 1; repeat from ★ across to last 13 chs, skip next ch, dc in next 9 chs, work ending decrease: 183 sts and 27 sps.

Row 2: Ch 3, turn; dc in next dc, ★ † decrease, dc in next 4 dc, work Cluster, dc in next ch-1 sp, work Cluster, (dc, ch 3, dc) in next ch-3 sp, work Cluster, dc in next ch-1 sp, work Cluster, skip next 2 dc, dc in next 4 dc, decrease †, skip next 2 dc; repeat from ★ 7 times **more**, then repeat from † to † once, work ending decrease: 36 Clusters and 9 ch-3 sps.

Row 3: Ch 3, turn; dc in next dc, ★ † decrease, dc in next 2 dc, (ch 2, skip next Cluster, dc in next dc) twice, ch 1, (dc, ch 3, dc) in next ch-3 sp, ch 1, (dc in next dc, ch 2, skip next Cluster) twice, dc in next 2 dc, decrease †, skip next 2 dc; repeat from ★ 7 times **more**, then repeat from † to † once, work ending decrease: 111 sts and 63 sps.

Row 4: Ch 3, turn; dc in next dc, ★ † decrease, 2 dc in next ch-2 sp, dc in next dc and in next ch-2 sp, work Cluster, dc in next ch-1 sp, work Cluster, (dc, ch 3, dc) in next ch-3 sp, work Cluster, dc in next ch-1 sp, work Cluster, dc in next ch-2 sp and in next dc, 2 dc in next ch-2 sp, decrease †, skip next 2 dc; repeat from ★ 7 times **more**, then repeat from † to † once, work ending decrease: 36 Clusters and 9 ch-3 sps.

Repeat Rows 3 and 4 until Afghan measures approximately 65" from beginning ch, ending by working Row 3.

Last Row: Ch 3, turn; dc in next dc, ★ † decrease, (2 dc in next ch-2 sp, dc in next dc) twice, dc in next ch-1 sp and in next dc, ch 1, (dc, ch 3, dc) in next ch-3 sp, ch 1, dc in next dc and in next ch-1 sp, (dc in next dc, 2 dc in next ch-2 sp) twice, decrease †, skip next 2 dc; repeat from ★ 7 times **more**, then repeat from † to † once, work ending decrease: 183 sts and 27 sps.

Edging: Ch 1, turn; slip st in first dc, ch 2, skip next dc, (slip st in next dc, ch 2, skip next dc) 4 times, slip st in next ch-1 sp, ch 2, (slip st, ch 2) twice in next ch-3 sp, skip next dc, slip st in next ch-1 sp, ch 2, ★ skip next dc, (slip st in next dc, ch 2, skip next dc) 3 times, slip st in next 4 dc, ch 2, skip next dc, (slip st in next dc, ch 2, skip next dc) 3 times, slip st in next ch-1 sp, ch 2, (slip st, ch 2) twice in next ch-3 sp, skip next dc, slip st in next ch-1 sp, ch 2; repeat from ★ 7 times **more**, (skip next dc, slip st in next dc, ch 2) 5 times, dc in same st; working in end of rows, skip first row, (slip st, ch 2, dc) in next row and in each row across to last row, skip last row; working in free loops and in sps of beginning ch *(Fig. 26b, page 142)*, slip st in marked ch, ch 2, (slip st in next ch, ch 2, skip next ch) 6 times, slip st in next 2 chs, ch 2, † skip next ch, (slip st in next ch, ch 2, skip next ch) 5 times, (slip st, ch 2) twice in next ch-2 sp, skip next ch, (slip st in next ch, ch 2, skip next ch) 5 times, slip st in next 2 chs, ch 2 †, repeat from † to † 7 times **more**, (skip next ch, slip st in next ch, ch 2) 6 times, (slip st, ch 2, dc) in next ch; working in end of rows, skip first row, (slip st, ch 2, dc) in next row and in each row across to last row, skip last row; join with slip st to first slip st, finish off.

SIMPLY KITTY

This afghan is simply the cat's meow! Worked in soft brushed acrylic yarn, it's terrific for cuddling. The feline silhouettes are formed with easy clusters, and tan and off-white yarns combine to mimic the coat of a tabby cat.

Finished Size: 53" x 70"

MATERIALS

Worsted Weight Brushed Acrylic Yarn:
   Tan - 42 ounces, (1,190 grams, 2,190 yards)
   Off-White - 34 ounces, (970 grams, 1,770 yards)
Crochet hook, size I (5.50 mm) **or** size needed
   for gauge

GAUGE: In pattern, sc, (ch 1, sc) 7 times and
         14 rows = 4"

Gauge Swatch: 4" square
Ch 16 **loosely.**
Row 1: Sc in second ch from hook, ★ ch 1, skip next ch, sc in next ch; repeat from ★ across: 8 sc and 7 ch-1 sps.
Rows 2-14: Ch 1, turn; sc in first sc, (ch 1, sc in next sc) across.
Finish off.

Note: Each row is worked across length of Afghan. When joining yarn and finishing off, always leave an 8" end to be worked into fringe.

STITCH GUIDE

> **CLUSTER**
> Ch 4, YO twice, insert hook in fourth ch from hook, YO and pull up a loop, (YO and draw through 2 loops on hook) twice, YO twice, insert hook in same ch, YO and pull up a loop, (YO and draw through 2 loops on hook) twice, YO and draw through all 3 loops on hook *(Fig. 15a, page 140)*.

AFGHAN BODY

With Off-White, ch 262 **loosely.**
Row 1 (Right side): Sc in second ch from hook, ★ ch 1, skip next ch, sc in next ch; repeat from ★ across; finish off: 131 sc and 130 ch-1 sps.
Note: Loop a short piece of yarn around any stitch to mark Row 1 as **right** side.

Row 2: With **wrong** side facing, join Tan with sc in first sc *(see Joining With Sc, page 142)*; (ch 1, sc in next sc) across; finish off.
Row 3: With **right** side facing, join Off-White with sc in first sc; (ch 1, sc in next sc) across; finish off.
Rows 4 and 5: Repeat Rows 2 and 3.
Row 6: With **wrong** side facing, join Tan with sc in first sc; (ch 1, sc in next sc) 24 times, work Cluster, skip next sc, sc in next sc, ★ (ch 1, sc in next sc) 32 times, work Cluster, skip next sc, sc in next sc; repeat from ★ 2 times **more**, (ch 1, sc in next sc) twice; finish off: 4 Clusters.

Note: When instructed to work into a skipped stitch **below** a Cluster, always work **behind** Cluster.

Row 7: With **right** side facing, join Off-White with sc in first sc; (ch 1, sc in next sc) twice, ch 1, dc in skipped sc one row **below** next Cluster, ★ ch 1, (sc in next sc, ch 1) 33 times, dc in skipped sc one row **below** next Cluster; repeat from ★ 2 times **more**, (ch 1, sc in next sc) across; finish off.
Row 8: With **wrong** side facing, join Tan with sc in first sc; (ch 1, sc in next sc) 22 times, (work Cluster, skip next st, sc in next sc) twice, ★ (ch 1, sc in next sc) 30 times, (work Cluster, skip next st, sc in next sc) twice; repeat from ★ 2 times **more**, (ch 1, sc in next sc) twice; finish off: 8 Clusters.
Row 9: With **right** side facing, join Off-White with sc in first sc; (ch 1, sc in next sc) twice, ch 1, dc in skipped dc one row **below** next Cluster, ch 1, sc in next sc, ch 1, dc in skipped sc one row **below** next Cluster, ★ (ch 1, sc in next sc) 31 times, ch 1, dc in skipped dc one row **below** next Cluster, ch 1, sc in next sc, ch 1, dc in skipped sc one row **below** next Cluster; repeat from ★ 2 times **more**, (ch 1, sc in next sc) across; finish off.
Row 10: With **wrong** side facing, join Tan with sc in first sc; (ch 1, sc in next sc) twice, (work Cluster, skip next sc, sc in next sc) 4 times, (ch 1, sc in next sc) twice, (work Cluster, skip next st, sc in next sc) 7 times, ★ (ch 1, sc in next sc) 10 times, (work Cluster, skip next sc, sc in next sc) 4 times, (ch 1, sc in next sc) twice, (work Cluster, skip next st, sc in next sc) 7 times; repeat from ★ 2 times **more**, (ch 1, sc in next sc) twice; finish off: 44 Clusters.

Continued on page 16.

Row 11: With **right** side facing, join Off-White with sc in first sc; (ch 1, sc in next sc) twice, ch 1, dc in skipped st one row **below** next Cluster, (ch 1, sc in next sc, ch 1, dc in skipped st one row **below** next Cluster) 6 times, (ch 1, sc in next sc) 3 times, ch 1, dc in skipped sc one row **below** next Cluster, (ch 1, sc in next sc, ch 1, dc in skipped st one row **below** next Cluster) 3 times, ★ (ch 1, sc in next sc) 11 times, ch 1, dc in skipped dc one row **below** next Cluster, (ch 1, sc in next sc, ch 1, dc in skipped st one row **below** next Cluster) 6 times, (ch 1, sc in next sc) 3 times, ch 1, dc in skipped sc one row **below** next Cluster, (ch 1, sc in next sc, ch 1, dc in skipped st one row **below** next Cluster) 3 times; repeat from ★ 2 times **more**, (ch 1, sc in next sc) across; finish off.

Row 12: With **wrong** side facing, join Tan with sc in first sc; (ch 1, sc in next st) 4 times, (work Cluster, skip next st, sc in next sc) 11 times, ★ (ch 1, skip next ch, sc in next st) 12 times, (work Cluster, skip next st, sc in next sc) 11 times; repeat from ★ 2 times **more**, (ch 1, sc in next sc) twice; finish off: 44 Clusters.

Row 13: With **right** side facing, join Off-White with sc in first sc; (ch 1, sc in next sc) twice, ch 1, dc in skipped dc one row **below** next Cluster, (ch 1, sc in next sc, ch 1, dc in skipped st one row **below** next Cluster) 10 times, ★ (ch 1, sc in next st) 13 times, ch 1, dc in skipped dc one row **below** next Cluster, (ch 1, sc in next sc, ch 1, dc in skipped st one row **below** next Cluster) 10 times; repeat from ★ 2 times **more**, (ch 1, sc in next sc) across; finish off.

Rows 14-19: Repeat Rows 12 and 13, 3 times.

Row 20: With **wrong** side facing, join Tan with sc in first sc; (ch 1, sc in next sc) twice, (work Cluster, skip next st, sc in next sc) 12 times, ★ (ch 1, sc in next sc) 10 times, (work Cluster, skip next st, sc in next sc) 12 times; repeat from ★ 2 times **more**, (ch 1, sc in next sc) twice; finish off: 48 Clusters.

Row 21: With **right** side facing, join Off-White with sc in first sc; (ch 1, sc in next sc) twice, ch 1, dc in skipped dc one row **below** next Cluster, (ch 1, sc in next sc, ch 1, dc in skipped st one row **below** next Cluster) 11 times, ★ (ch 1, sc in next sc) 11 times, ch 1, dc in skipped dc one row **below** next Cluster, (ch 1, sc in next sc, ch 1, dc in skipped st one row **below** next Cluster) 11 times; repeat from ★ 2 times **more**, (ch 1, sc in next sc) across; finish off.

Row 22: With **wrong** side facing, join Tan with sc in first sc; (ch 1, skip next ch, sc in next st) 10 times, (work Cluster, skip next dc, sc in next sc) 8 times, ★ (ch 1, skip next ch, sc in next st) 18 times, (work Cluster, skip next dc, sc in next sc) 8 times; repeat from ★ 2 times **more**, (ch 1, sc in next sc) twice; finish off: 32 Clusters.

Row 23: With **right** side facing, join Off-White with sc in first sc; (ch 1, sc in next sc) twice, ch 1, dc in skipped dc one row **below** next Cluster, (ch 1, sc in next sc, ch 1, dc in skipped dc one row **below** next Cluster) 7 times, ★ (ch 1, sc in next sc) 19 times, ch 1, dc in skipped dc one row **below** next Cluster, (ch 1, sc in next sc, ch 1, dc in skipped dc one row **below** next Cluster) 7 times; repeat from ★ 2 times **more**, (ch 1, sc in next sc) across; finish off.

Rows 24 and 25: Repeat Rows 22 and 23.

Row 26: With **wrong** side facing, join Tan with sc in first sc; (ch 1, skip next ch, sc in next st) 12 times, (work Cluster, skip next dc, sc in next sc) 7 times, ★ (ch 1, skip next ch, sc in next st) 20 times, (work Cluster, skip next dc, sc in next sc) 7 times; repeat from ★ 2 times **more**, (ch 1, sc in next sc) twice; finish off: 28 Clusters.

Row 27: With **right** side facing, join Off-White with sc in first sc; (ch 1, sc in next sc) twice, ch 1, dc in skipped dc one row **below** next Cluster, (ch 1, sc in next sc, ch 1, dc in skipped dc one row **below** next Cluster) 6 times, ★ (ch 1, sc in next sc) 21 times, ch 1, dc in skipped dc one row **below** next Cluster, (ch 1, sc in next sc, ch 1, dc in skipped dc one row **below** next Cluster) 6 times; repeat from ★ 2 times **more**, (ch 1, sc in next sc) across; finish off.

Rows 28 and 29: Repeat Rows 26 and 27.

Row 30: With **wrong** side facing, join Tan with sc in first sc; (ch 1, skip next ch, sc in next st) 14 times, (work Cluster, skip next dc, sc in next sc) 6 times, ★ (ch 1, skip next ch, sc in next st) 22 times, (work Cluster, skip next dc, sc in next sc) 6 times; repeat from ★ 2 times **more**, (ch 1, sc in next sc) twice; finish off: 24 Clusters.

Row 31: With **right** side facing, join Off-White with sc in first sc; (ch 1, sc in next sc) twice, ch 1, dc in skipped dc one row **below** next Cluster, (ch 1, sc in next sc, ch 1, dc in skipped dc one row **below** next Cluster) 5 times, ★ (ch 1, sc in next sc) 23 times, ch 1, dc in skipped dc one row **below** next Cluster, (ch 1, sc in next sc, ch 1, dc in skipped dc one row **below** next Cluster) 5 times; repeat from ★ 2 times **more**, (ch 1, sc in next sc) across; finish off.

Row 32: With **wrong** side facing, join Tan with sc in first sc; (ch 1, skip next ch, sc in next st) 16 times, (work Cluster, skip next dc, sc in next sc) 5 times, ★ (ch 1, skip next ch, sc in next st) 24 times, (work Cluster, skip next dc, sc in next sc) 5 times; repeat from ★ 2 times **more**, (ch 1, sc in next sc) twice; finish off: 20 Clusters.

Row 33: With **right** side facing, join Off-White with sc in first sc; (ch 1, sc in next sc) twice, ch 1, dc in skipped dc one row **below** next Cluster, (ch 1, sc in next sc, ch 1, dc in skipped dc one row **below** next Cluster) 4 times, ★ (ch 1, sc in next sc) 25 times, ch 1, dc in skipped dc one row **below** next Cluster, (ch 1, sc in next sc, ch 1, dc in skipped dc one row **below** next Cluster) 4 times; repeat from ★ 2 times **more**, (ch 1, sc in next sc) across; finish off.

Row 34: With **wrong** side facing, join Tan with sc in first sc; (ch 1, skip next ch, sc in next st) 23 times, work Cluster, skip next sc, sc in next dc, ★ (ch 1, skip next ch, sc in next st) 32 times, work Cluster, skip next sc, sc in next dc; repeat from ★ 2 times **more**, (ch 1, sc in next sc) across; finish off: 4 Clusters.

Row 35: With **right** side facing, join Off-White with sc in first sc; (ch 1, sc in next sc) 3 times, ch 1, dc in skipped sc one row **below** next Cluster, ★ (ch 1, sc in next sc) 33 times, ch 1, dc in skipped sc one row **below** next Cluster; repeat from ★ 2 times **more**, (ch 1, sc in next sc) across; finish off.

Row 36: With **wrong** side facing, join Tan with sc in first sc; (ch 1, sc in next sc) 22 times, work Cluster, skip next sc, sc in next dc, ★ (ch 1, sc in next sc) 32 times, work Cluster, skip next sc, sc in next dc; repeat from ★ 2 times **more**, (ch 1, sc in next sc) across; finish off: 4 Clusters.

Row 37: With **right** side facing, join Off-White with sc in first sc; (ch 1, sc in next sc) 4 times, ch 1, dc in skipped sc one row **below** next Cluster, ★ (ch 1, sc in next sc) 33 times, ch 1, dc in skipped sc one row **below** next Cluster; repeat from ★ 2 times **more**, (ch 1, sc in next sc) across; finish off.

Row 38: With **wrong** side facing, join Tan with sc in first sc; (ch 1, sc in next sc) 13 times, (work Cluster, skip next sc, sc in next st) 5 times, ★ (ch 1, sc in next sc) 24 times, (work Cluster, skip next sc, sc in next st) 5 times; repeat from ★ 2 times **more**, (ch 1, sc in next sc) across; finish off: 20 Clusters.

Row 39: With **right** side facing, join Off-White with sc in first sc; (ch 1, sc in next sc) 5 times, ch 1, dc in skipped sc one row **below** next Cluster, (ch 1, sc in next sc, ch 1, dc in skipped sc one row **below** next Cluster) 4 times, ★ (ch 1, sc in next sc) 25 times, ch 1, dc in skipped sc one row **below** next Cluster, (ch 1, sc in next sc, ch 1, dc in skipped sc one row **below** next Cluster) 4 times; repeat from ★ 2 times **more**, (ch 1, sc in next sc) across; finish off.

Row 40: With **wrong** side facing, join Tan with sc in first sc; (ch 1, sc in next sc) 12 times, work Cluster, skip next sc, sc in next dc, ★ (ch 1, skip next ch, sc in next st) 32 times, work Cluster, skip next sc, sc in next dc; repeat from ★ 2 times **more**, (ch 1, skip next ch, sc in next st) across; finish off: 4 Clusters.

Row 41: With **right** side facing, join Off-White with sc in first sc; (ch 1, sc in next sc) 14 times, ch 1, dc in skipped sc one row **below** next Cluster, ★ (ch 1, sc in next sc) 33 times, ch 1, dc in skipped sc one row **below** next Cluster; repeat from ★ 2 times **more**, (ch 1, sc in next sc) across; finish off.

Row 42: With **wrong** side facing, join Tan with sc in first sc; (ch 1, skip next ch, sc in next st) across; finish off.

Row 43: With **right** side facing, join Off-White with sc in first sc; (ch 1, sc in next sc) across; finish off.

Rows 44-51: Repeat Rows 42 and 43, 4 times.

Rows 52-179: Repeat Rows 6-51 twice, then repeat Rows 6-41 once **more**.

Rows 180-183: Repeat Rows 42 and 43 twice.

EDGING

FIRST SIDE

With **right** side facing and working across sts on Row 183, join Off-White with slip st in first sc; slip st in next ch-1 sp, (ch 1, slip st in next ch-1 sp) across to last sc, slip st in last sc; finish off.

SECOND SIDE

With **right** side facing, join Off-White with slip st in free loop of first ch *(Fig. 26b, page 142)*; working in sps of beginning ch, slip st in next sp, (ch 1, slip st in next sp) across to last ch, slip st in free loop of last ch; finish off.

Holding 2 strands of corresponding color together, add additional fringe in each row across short edges of Afghan *(Figs. 31b & d, page 143)*.

VICTORIAN LACE

Fashioned in shades of purple, this regal wrap is befitting of royalty! The Victorian throw, crocheted in strips, gets its lacy scallops from a combination of double and treble cluster stitches.

STITCH GUIDE

DOUBLE CROCHET CLUSTER *(abbreviated dc Cluster)*
★ YO, insert hook in st indicated, YO and pull up a loop, YO and draw through 2 loops on hook; repeat from ★ 2 times **more**, YO and draw through all 4 loops on hook *(Fig. 15a, page 140)*.

BEGINNING DOUBLE CROCHET CLUSTER
 (abbreviated beginning dc Cluster)
Ch 2, ★ YO, insert hook in st indicated, YO and pull up a loop, YO and draw through 2 loops on hook; repeat from ★ once **more**, YO and draw through all 3 loops on hook.

TREBLE CROCHET CLUSTER *(abbreviated tr Cluster)*
★ YO twice, insert hook in st indicated, YO and pull up a loop, (YO and draw through 2 loops on hook) twice; repeat from ★ 2 times **more**, YO and draw through all 4 loops on hook.

FIRST STRIP
CENTER
Row 1 (Right side)**:** With Lt Purple, ch 4, work dc Cluster in fourth ch from hook.

Note: Loop a short piece of yarn around any stitch to mark Row 1 as **right** side and bottom edge.

Rows 2-77: Ch 4, turn; work dc Cluster in fourth ch from hook. Do **not** finish off.

BORDER
Rnd 1: Ch 1, do **not** turn; sc in dc Cluster just made, † ch 4; working in end of rows, sc in first row, (ch 3, sc in next row) 76 times, ch 4 †, sc in free loop of beginning ch *(Fig. 26b, page 142)*, repeat from † to † once; join with slip st to first sc, finish off: 156 sps.

Rnd 2: With **right** side facing and beginning at bottom edge, join Purple with slip st in first ch-4 sp; ch 3 **(counts as first dc, now and throughout)**, 4 dc in same sp, † dc in next sc, 5 dc in next ch-4 sp, ch 1, sc in next ch-3 sp, ch 1, ★ 3 dc in each of next 2 ch-3 sps, ch 1, sc in next ch-3 sp, ch 1; repeat from ★ 24 times **more** †, 5 dc in next ch-4 sp, repeat from † to † once; join with slip st to first dc, do **not** finish off: 322 dc.

Continued on page 27.

Finished Size: 50" x 65"

MATERIALS
  Worsted Weight Yarn:
    Purple - 23 ounces,
      (650 grams, 1,575 yards)
    Dk Purple - 14 ounces,
      (400 grams, 960 yards)
    Lt Purple - 10 ounces,
      (280 grams, 685 yards)
  Crochet hook, size H (5.00 mm) **or** size needed for gauge

GAUGE: Each Strip = 5" wide

HEARTWARMING FANS

*With its pretty border of hearts, this sweet throw is
extra special. Fanciful fans give the heartwarming afghan
a lacy look that will be enjoyed any time of the year.*

Finished Size: 48" x 64"

MATERIALS
Worsted Weight Yarn:
  Ecru - 35 ounces, (990 grams, 2,400 yards)
  Dk Rose - 2 ounces, (60 grams, 135 yards)
  Rose - 1 1/2 ounces, (40 grams, 105 yards)
Crochet hook, size H (5.00 mm) **or** size needed
  for gauge

GAUGE: In pattern, 2 repeats and Rows 1-7 = 4"
        Each Heart = 5 3/4"w

Gauge Swatch: 5 1/2"w x 4"h
Ch 27 **loosely**.
Work same as Afghan for 7 rows.
Finish off.

STITCH GUIDE

> **CLUSTER** (uses next 5 sts)
> ★ YO, insert hook in **next** ch or dc, YO and pull up a loop,
> YO and draw through 2 loops on hook; repeat from ★ 4 times
> **more**, YO and draw through all 6 loops on hook *(Fig. 15b, page 140)*.

AFGHAN BODY
With Ecru, ch 187 **loosely**, place marker in third ch from hook
for st placement.
Row 1 (Right side)**:** 5 Dc in seventh ch from hook **(6 skipped
chs count as first dc plus 3 skipped chs)**, ★ skip next
3 chs, (dc, ch 2, dc) in next ch, skip next 3 chs, 5 dc in next ch;
repeat from ★ across to last 4 chs, skip next 3 chs, dc in last ch:
161 dc and 22 ch-2 sps.
Note: Loop a short piece of yarn around any stitch to mark
Row 1 as **right** side.
Row 2: Ch 3 **(counts as first dc, now and throughout)**,
turn; skip next 2 dc, (dc, ch 2, dc) in next dc, ★ 5 dc in next
ch-2 sp, skip next 3 dc, (dc, ch 2, dc) in next dc; repeat from ★
across to last 3 dc, skip next 2 dc, dc in last dc: 158 dc and
23 ch-2 sps.

Row 3: Ch 3, turn; 5 dc in next ch-2 sp, ★ skip next 3 dc, (dc,
ch 2, dc) in next dc, 5 dc in next ch-2 sp; repeat from ★ across
to last 2 dc, skip next dc, dc in last dc: 161 dc and 22 ch-2 sps.
Rows 4-13: Repeat Rows 2 and 3, 5 times.
Row 14: Ch 1, turn; sc in each dc and in each ch-2 sp across:
183 sc.
Rows 15-18: Ch 1, turn; sc in each sc across.
Row 19: Ch 3, turn; skip next 2 sc, 5 dc in next sc, ★ skip next
3 sc, (dc, ch 2, dc) in next sc, skip next 3 sc, 5 dc in next sc;
repeat from ★ across to last 3 sc, skip next 2 sc, dc in last sc:
161 dc and 22 ch-2 sps.
Rows 20-31: Repeat Rows 2 and 3, 6 times.
Rows 32-105: Repeat Rows 14-31, 4 times; then repeat
Rows 14 and 15 once **more**.
Finish off.

BOTTOM EDGING
Row 1: With **wrong** side facing and working in free loops of
beginning ch *(Fig. 26b, page 142)*, join Ecru with sc in
marked ch *(see Joining With Sc, page 142)*; work 182 sc
evenly spaced across: 183 sc.
Row 2: Ch 1, turn; sc in each sc across; finish off.

HEART PANEL (Make 2)
FIRST HEART
With Dk Rose, ch 18 **loosely**.
Rnd 1 (Right side)**:** 2 Dc in fourth ch from hook **(3 skipped
chs count as first dc)** and in next ch, dc in next 3 chs, work
Cluster, dc in next 3 chs, 2 dc in next ch, 5 dc in last ch;
working in free loops of beginning ch, 2 dc in next ch, dc in
next 5 chs, 5 dc in next ch, dc in next 5 chs, 2 dc in next ch and
in same ch as first dc; join with slip st to first dc: 40 sts.
Note: Mark Rnd 1 as **right** side.
Rnd 2: Ch 3, dc in same st, 2 dc in each of next 2 dc, dc in next
3 dc, work Cluster, dc in next 3 dc, 2 dc in each of next 5 dc, dc
in next 9 dc, 5 dc in next dc, dc in next 9 dc, 2 dc in each of last
2 dc; join with slip st to first dc, finish off: 50 sts.

Continued on page 26.

Rnd 3: With **right** side facing, join Ecru with sc in same st as joining; (ch 3, skip next dc, sc in next dc) 14 times, place marker around last ch-3 made for joining placement, (ch 3, skip next dc, sc in next dc) twice, ch 3, skip next dc, (sc, ch 3) twice in next dc, skip next dc, (sc in next dc, ch 3, skip next dc) around; join with slip st to first sc, finish off.

SECOND HEART

With Rose, work same as First Heart through Rnd 2: 50 sts.
Rnd 3 (Joining rnd): With **right** side facing, join Ecru with sc in same st as joining; (ch 3, skip next st, sc in next dc) 9 times, ch 1, with **wrong** sides together, sc in marked ch-3 sp on **previous Heart** *(Fig. 29, page 142)*, ch 1, skip next dc on **new Heart**, (sc in next dc, ch 1, sc in next ch-3 sp on **previous Heart**, ch 1, skip next dc on **new Heart**) 4 times, (sc in next dc, ch 3, skip next dc) 3 times, (sc, ch 3) twice in next dc, skip next dc, (sc in next dc, ch 3, skip next dc) across, place marker in last ch-3 made for joining placement; join with slip st to first sc, finish off.

THIRD HEART

Work same as First Heart through Rnd 2: 50 sts.
Rnd 3 (Joining rnd): With **right** side facing, join Ecru with sc in same st as joining; (ch 3, skip next dc, sc in next dc) 14 times, place marker around last ch-3 made for joining placement, (ch 3, skip next dc, sc in next dc) twice, ch 3, skip next dc, (sc, ch 3) twice in next dc, skip next dc, sc in next dc, (ch 3, skip next dc, sc in next dc) twice, ch 1, with **wrong** sides together, sc in marked ch-3 sp on **previous Heart**, ch 1, skip next dc on **new Heart**, (sc in next dc, ch 1, sc in next ch-3 sp on **previous Heart**, ch 1, skip next dc on **next Heart**) 4 times; join with slip st to first sc, finish off.

FOURTH THRU NINTH HEARTS

Repeat Second and Third Hearts, 3 times.

EDGING

Row 1 (Right side): With **right** side facing, join Ecru with slip st in first ch-3 sp to left of joining on First Heart; ch 5, (sc in next ch-3 sp, ch 2) twice, dc in next ch-3 sp, ch 2, skip next ch-3 sp, dc in next ch-3 sp, ch 2, (sc in next ch-3 sp, ch 2) twice, dc in next ch-3 sp, ★ ch 2, skip next joining, tr in next ch-3 sp on **next Heart**, ch 2, dc in next ch-3 sp, ch 2, skip next ch-3 sp, sc in next ch-3 sp (at point), ch 2, skip next ch-3 sp, dc in next ch-3 sp, ch 2, tr in next ch-3 sp, ch 2, skip next joining, dc in next ch-3 sp on **next Heart**, ch 2, (sc in next ch-3 sp, ch 2) twice, dc in next ch-3 sp, ch 2, skip next ch-3 sp, dc in next ch-3 sp, ch 2, (sc in next ch-3 sp, ch 2) twice, dc in next ch-3 sp; repeat from ★ across.
Row 2: Ch 1, turn; work 183 sc evenly spaced across; finish off.

JOINING

With **right** sides of short edge of Afghan Body and long edge of Heart Panel held together, and working through **both** thicknesses, join Ecru with sc in first sc; sc in next sc and in each sc across; finish off.
Repeat for second edge.

BORDER

With **right** side of long edge facing and working in end of rows, join Ecru with sc in end of Joining; † ch 3, skip next 2 rows, (sc in next row, ch 3) 13 times, skip next 2 rows, [sc in next row, ch 3, skip next 2 rows, (sc in next row, ch 3) 13 times, skip next 2 rows] 5 times, sc in Joining, ch 3, skip next 2 rows, sc in next row, ch 3, working around Heart Panel, (sc in next ch-3 sp, ch 3) 13 times, sc in next 2 sps, ch 3, (sc in next ch-3 sp, ch 3) 4 times, sc in next 2 ch-3 sps, ch 3, (sc in next ch-3 sp, ch 3) 3 times, sc in next 2 sps, ★ ch 3, (sc in next ch-3 sp, ch 3) 7 times, sc in next 2 sps, ch 3, (sc in next ch-3 sp, ch 3) 4 times, sc in next 2 sps, ch 3, (sc in next ch-3 sp, ch 3) 3 times, sc in next 2 sps; repeat from ★ 2 times **more**, ch 3, (sc in next ch-3 sp, ch 3) 13 times; working in end of rows, sc in next row, ch 3, skip next 2 rows †, sc in Joining, repeat from † to † once; join with slip st to first sc, finish off.

VICTORIAN LACE Continued from page 18.

Rnd 3: Slip st in next dc, work beginning dc Cluster in same st, † ch 5, (skip next dc, work tr Cluster in next dc, ch 5) 3 times, skip next dc, work dc Cluster in next dc, ch 3, sc in next sc, ★ ch 3, skip next dc, work dc Cluster in next dc, ch 3, skip next dc, work tr Cluster in next dc, ch 3, skip next dc, work dc Cluster in next dc, ch 3, sc in next sc; repeat from ★ 24 times **more**, ch 3 †, skip next dc, work dc Cluster in next dc, repeat from † to † once; join with slip st to top of beginning dc Cluster, finish off: 160 Clusters and 212 sps.

Rnd 4: With **right** side facing, join Dk Purple with slip st in first ch-5 sp; ch 1, 6 sc in same sp and in each of next 3 ch-5 sps, † 2 sc in each of next 2 ch-3 sps, ★ 4 sc in each of next 2 ch-3 sps, 2 sc in each of next 2 ch-3 sps; repeat from ★ 24 times **more** †, 6 sc in each of next 4 ch-5 sps, repeat from † to † once; join with slip st to first sc: 656 sc.

Rnd 5: Ch 1, sc in same st, † (ch 2, skip next sc, sc in next sc) 12 times, skip next sc, slip st in next sc, ★ skip next sc, sc in next sc, (ch 2, skip next sc, sc in next sc) 4 times, skip next sc, slip st in next sc; repeat from ★ 24 times **more**, skip next sc †, sc in next sc, repeat from † to † once; join with slip st to first sc, finish off.

REMAINING 9 STRIPS

Work same as First Strip through Rnd 4 of Border: 656 sc.

Rnd 5 (Joining rnd): Ch 1, sc in same st, (ch 2, skip next sc, sc in next sc) 12 times, skip next sc, slip st in next sc, skip next sc, sc in next sc, ★ (ch 2, skip next sc, sc in next sc) 4 times, skip next sc, slip st in next sc, skip next sc, sc in next sc; repeat from ★ 24 times **more**, (ch 2, skip next sc, sc in next sc) 12 times, skip next sc, slip st in next sc, skip next sc, sc in next sc, ch 2, skip next sc, sc in next sc, ch 1, holding Strips with **wrong** sides together and bottom edges at same end, slip st in corresponding ch-2 sp on **previous Strip** *(Fig. 29, page 142)*, ch 1, skip next sc on **new Strip**, sc in next sc, ch 1, slip st in corresponding ch-2 sp on **previous Strip**, ch 1, skip next sc on **new Strip**, sc in next sc, ch 2, skip next sc, sc in next sc, skip next sc, slip st in next sc, skip next sc, † sc in next sc, ch 2, skip next sc, sc in next sc, (ch 1, slip st in corresponding ch-2 sp on **previous Strip**, ch 1, skip next sc on **new Strip**, sc in next sc) twice, ch 2, skip next sc, sc in next sc, skip next sc, slip st in next sc, skip next sc †, repeat from † to † across; join with slip st to first sc, finish off.

CUPID'S DREAM Continued from page 22.

Row 21: Repeat Row 11.
Row 22: Repeat Row 14.
Row 23: Repeat Row 11.
Row 24: Changing to Dk Rose, repeat Row 14.
Row 25: Repeat Row 11.
Rows 26-29: Repeat Rows 10 and 11 twice.
Rows 30-93: Repeat Rows 14-29, 4 times.
Rows 94-98: Turn; slip st in first 3 dc and in ch-3 sp of first Block, ch 3, 3 dc in same sp, work Blocks across to last Block, slip st in ch-3 sp of last Block: 3 Blocks.
Row 99: Turn; slip st in first 3 dc and in ch-3 sp of first Block, ch 3, 3 dc in same sp, work Block, slip st in ch-3 sp of last Block: 2 Blocks.
Row 100: Turn; slip st in first 3 dc and in ch-3 sp of first Block, ch 3, 3 dc in same sp, slip st in ch-3 sp of last Block; finish off: 1 Block.

ASSEMBLY

Place two Strips together with bottom edges at the same end and alternating **right** side of first Strip with **wrong** side of second Strip. With corresponding colors and being careful to match stripes, sew Strips together.
Repeat to join remaining Strips.

EDGING
FOUNDATION RND

With **right** side facing and beginning at top left corner, join Dk Rose with slip st in top of beginning ch-3 of corner Block; ch 1, sc in same st (corner), ch 2, (sc in next sp between Blocks, ch 2) across to next corner Block, ★ sc in corner, ch 2, (sc in next sp between Blocks, ch 2) across to next corner Block; repeat from ★ 2 times **more**; join with slip st to first sc, do **not** finish off.

FIRST SIDE

Ch 3, 3 dc in next ch-2 sp and in each ch-2 sp across to next corner sc, ch 3, slip st in corner sc; finish off.

SECOND SIDE

With **right** side facing, join Dk Rose with slip st in bottom right corner sc; work in same manner as First Side.

Holding 3 strands of each color together, add fringe evenly across short edges of Afghan *(Figs. 31a-d, page 143)*.

CLIMBING ROSES

Like your own secret garden, this glorious throw will draw you to linger near a sunny window. Worked in single crochet and front post treble stitches, it was inspired by the beauty of climbing roses.

Finished Size: 46" x 56"

MATERIALS
Worsted Weight Yarn:
  Ecru - 14 ounces,
    (400 grams, 960 yards)
  Rose - 8 ounces,
    (230 grams, 550 yards)
  Green - 8 ounces,
    (230 grams, 550 yards)
  Lt Green - 7 ounces,
    (200 grams, 480 yards)
  Lt Rose - 7 ounces,
    (200 grams, 480 yards)
Crochet hook, size J (6.00 mm) **or** size
  needed for gauge

GAUGE: In pattern,
    10 sts and 13 rows = 3¹/₂"

Gauge Swatch: 7"w x 3¹/₂"h
Ch 21 **loosely**.
Work same as Afghan for 13 rows.
Finish off.

STITCH GUIDE

FRONT POST TREBLE CROCHET (abbreviated FPtr)
YO twice, insert hook from **front** to **back** around post of st indicated, YO and pull up a loop *(Fig. 12, page 139)*, (YO and draw through 2 loops on hook) 3 times. Skip sc behind FPtr.

With Ecru, ch 132 **loosely**.
Row 1: Sc in second ch from hook and in each ch across: 131 sc.
Row 2 (Right side)**:** Ch 1, turn; sc in each sc across; finish off.
Note: Loop a short piece of yarn around any stitch to mark Row 2 as **right** side.
Row 3: With **right** side facing, join Rose with sc in first sc *(see Joining With Sc, page 142)*; sc in each sc across; finish off.
Row 4: With **wrong** side facing, join Green with sc in first sc; sc in each sc across; finish off.
Row 5: With **right** side facing, join Lt Green with sc in first sc; sc in each sc across; finish off.
Row 6: With **right** side facing, join Ecru with sc in first sc; sc in next sc, ★ work FPtr around sc 3 rows **below** next sc, sc in next 2 sc; repeat from ★ across; do **not** finish off: 43 FPtr.
Row 7: Ch 1, turn; sc in each st across; finish off: 131 sc.
Row 8: With **right** side facing, join Lt Green with sc in first sc; sc in each sc across; finish off.
Row 9: With **right** side facing, join Green with sc in first sc; sc in next sc, (work FPtr around FPtr 2 rows **below** next sc, sc in next 2 sc) across; finish off: 43 FPtr.
Row 10: With **wrong** side facing, join Rose with sc in first sc; sc in each st across; finish off: 131 sc.
Row 11: With **right** side facing, join Lt Rose with sc in first sc; sc in each sc across; finish off.
Row 12: With **right** side facing, join Ecru with sc in first sc; sc in next sc, (work FPtr around FPtr 2 rows **below** next sc, sc in next 2 sc) across; do **not** finish off: 43 FPtr.
Row 13: Ch 1, turn; sc in each st across; finish off: 131 sc.
Row 14: With **right** side facing, join Lt Rose with sc in first sc; sc in each sc across; finish off.
Row 15: With **right** side facing, join Rose with sc in first sc; sc in next sc, (work FPtr around FPtr 2 rows **below** next sc, sc in next 2 sc) across; finish off: 43 FPtr.

Row 16: With **wrong** side facing, join Green with sc in first sc; sc in each st across; finish off: 131 sc.

Row 17: With **right** side facing, join Lt Green with sc in first sc; sc in each sc across; finish off.

Row 18: With **right** side facing, join Ecru with sc in first sc; sc in next sc, (work FPtr around FPtr 2 rows **below** next sc, sc in next 2 sc) across; do **not** finish off: 43 FPtr.

Rows 19-207: Repeat Rows 7-18, 15 times; then repeat Rows 7-15 once **more**.

Row 208: With **wrong** side facing, join Ecru with sc in first sc; sc in each sc across; do **not** finish off.

Row 209: Ch 1, turn; sc in each sc across; finish off.

LACY CHARM

Lacy charm describes this mile-a-minute afghan, which works up quickly in strips using worsted weight yarn. Fashioned in ecru, the comforter will add a feminine touch wherever it's displayed.

Finished Size: 47" x 56"

MATERIALS
Worsted Weight Yarn:
32 ounces, (910 grams, 2,025 yards)
Crochet hook, size J (6.00 mm) **or** size needed
for gauge

GAUGE: 12 sc = 4"
Each Strip = 5¼" wide

STITCH GUIDE

> **PICOT**
> Ch 3, slip st in top of dc just made.

FIRST STRIP

Ch 152 **loosely**.

Foundation Row (Right side)**:** Sc in back ridge of second ch from hook and each ch across *(Fig. 2b, page 137)*: 151 sc.
Note: Loop a short piece of yarn around any stitch to mark Foundation Row as **right** side.
Rnd 1: Ch 5, skip end of Foundation Row; working in free loops of beginning ch *(Fig. 26b, page 142)*, slip st in first ch, ch 5, (skip next ch, slip st in next ch, ch 5) 75 times, skip end of Foundation Row; working across sc on Foundation Row, slip st in first sc, (ch 5, skip next sc, slip st in next sc) across; join with slip st to base of beginning ch-5: 152 ch-5 sps.
Rnd 2: Slip st in first ch-5 sp, † [ch 1, (dc, ch 1) twice, slip st] 3 times in same sp, ch 1, (dc, ch 1) twice in next ch-5 sp, ★ slip st in next ch-5 sp, ch 1, (dc, ch 1) twice in next ch-5 sp; repeat from ★ 36 times **more** †, slip st in next ch-5 sp, repeat from † to † once; join with slip st to first slip st: 246 ch-1 sps.

Rnd 3: Slip st in next ch, slip st in next dc and in next ch-1 sp, ch 3 **(counts as first dc)**, 4 dc in same sp, † ch 1, skip next 2 ch-1 sps, 6 dc in next ch-1 sp, ch 1, skip next 2 ch-1 sps, 5 dc in next ch-1 sp, ch 1, skip next 2 ch-1 sps, ★ 3 dc in next ch-1 sp, ch 1, skip next 2 ch-1 sps; repeat from ★ 37 times **more** †, 5 dc in next ch-1 sp, repeat from † to † once; join with slip st to first dc: 260 dc and 82 ch-1 sps.
Rnd 4: Ch 1, sc in same st, † hdc in next dc, 3 dc in next dc, hdc in next dc, sc in next dc, ch 1, slip st in next ch-1 sp, ch 1, dc in next dc, ch 1, (dc in next dc, work Picot) 4 times, ch 1, dc in next dc, ch 1, slip st in next ch-1 sp, ch 1, sc in next dc, hdc in next dc, 3 dc in next dc, hdc in next dc, sc in next dc, ch 1, slip st in next ch-1 sp, ch 1, ★ (dc, ch 1) twice in center dc of next 3-dc group, slip st in next ch-1 sp, ch 1; repeat from ★ 37 times **more** †, sc in next dc, repeat from † to † once; join with slip st to first sc, finish off: 244 ch-1 sps.

REMAINING 8 STRIPS

Work same as First Strip through Rnd 3: 260 dc and 82 ch-1 sps.
Rnd 4 (Joining rnd): Ch 1, sc in same st, † hdc in next dc, 3 dc in next dc, hdc in next dc, sc in next dc, ch 1, slip st in next ch-1 sp, ch 1, dc in next dc, ch 1, (dc in next dc, work Picot) 4 times, ch 1, dc in next dc, ch 1, slip st in next ch-1 sp, ch 1, sc in next dc, hdc in next dc, 3 dc in next dc, hdc in next dc, sc in next dc, ch 1, slip st in next ch-1 sp †, ch 1, [(dc, ch 1) twice in center dc of next 3-dc group, slip st in next ch-1 sp, ch 1] 38 times, sc in next dc, repeat from † to † once, ch 1, ★ dc in center dc of next 3-dc group, holding Strips with **wrong** sides together, sc in corresponding ch-1 sp on **previous Strip** *(Fig. 29, page 142)*, dc in same st on **new Strip**, ch 1, slip st in next ch-1 sp, ch 1; repeat from ★ across; join with slip st to first sc, finish off.

BABY'S CIRCLE OF LOVE

*Encircle your little one in love with this precious wrap.
Crocheted with sport weight yarn, it features strips of circles
joined by delicate openwork borders and a picot edging.*

Finished Size: 36" x 47"

MATERIALS
Sport Weight Yarn:
  18½ ounces, (530 grams, 1,745 yards)
Crochet hook, size F (3.75 mm) **or** size needed
  for gauge

GAUGE: Each Circle = 1½" in diameter
  Each Strip = 3½" wide

STITCH GUIDE

> **PICOT**
> Ch 4, sc in fourth ch from hook.
> **DECREASE**
> YO, insert hook in same sp, YO and pull up a loop, YO and
> draw through 2 loops on hook, YO, insert hook in next
> joining sc, YO and pull up a loop, YO and draw through
> 2 loops on hook, YO, insert hook in next ch-5 sp on next
> Strip, YO and pull up a loop, YO and draw through 2 loops
> on hook, YO and draw through all 4 loops on hook.

FIRST STRIP
CENTER
FIRST CIRCLE
Ch 4, dc in fourth ch from hook to form a ring.
Rnd 1 (Right side): Ch 3 **(counts as first dc, now and
throughout)**, 17 dc in ring; join with slip st to first dc, do **not**
finish off: 18 dc.
Note: Loop a short piece of yarn around any stitch to mark
Rnd 1 as **right** side and bottom edge.

REMAINING 28 CIRCLES
Note: When working remaining Circles, keep unworked ch-3
between Circles to **wrong** side.
Ch 7, dc in fourth ch from hook to form next ring.
Rnd 1 (Right side): Ch 3, 8 dc in ring, skip ch-3, 9 dc in ring;
join with slip to first dc, do **not** finish off: 18 dc.
Note: Mark Rnd 1 as **right** side.

BORDER
Note: Work into Circles with **right** side of each Circle facing at
all times.

Rnd 1: Ch 1, sc in same st as joining, (ch 3, skip next dc, sc in
next dc) 4 times, skip next dc after joining on next Circle, sc in
next dc, † (ch 3, skip next dc, sc in next dc) 3 times, skip next
dc after joining on next Circle, sc in next dc †, repeat from
† to † 26 times **more**, (ch 3, skip next dc, sc in next dc) 8
times, ★ skip next 2 dc after last sc worked on next Circle, sc in
next dc, (ch 3, skip next dc, sc in next dc) 3 times; repeat from
★ across to last Circle, skip next dc after last sc worked on last
Circle, (sc in next dc, ch 3, skip next dc) 4 times; join with
slip st to first sc: 178 ch-3 sps.
Rnd 2: Slip st in first ch-3 sp, ch 5, dc in same sp, ch 2, (dc,
ch 2) twice in next ch-3 sp, (dc in next ch-3 sp, ch 2) 85 times,
(dc, ch 2) twice in each of next 4 ch-3 sps, (dc in next ch-3 sp,
ch 2) across to last 2 ch-3 sps, (dc, ch 2) twice in each of last
2 ch-3 sps; join with slip st to third ch of beginning ch-5:
186 ch-2 sps.
Rnd 3: Slip st in first ch-2 sp, ch 1, sc in same sp, (ch 3, sc in
next ch-2 sp) around, ch 1, hdc in first sc to form last ch-3 sp.
Rnd 4: Ch 1, sc in same sp, ch 5, (sc in next ch-3 sp, ch 5)
around; join with slip st to first sc, finish off.

REMAINING 9 STRIPS
Work same as First Strip through Rnd 3 of Border: 186 ch-3 sps.
Rnd 4 (Joining rnd): Ch 1, sc in same sp, (ch 5, sc in next
ch-3 sp) 95 times, holding Strips with **wrong** sides together and
bottom edges at same end, ★ ch 2, sc in corresponding ch-5 sp
on **previous Strip** *(Fig. 29, page 142)*, ch 2, sc in next
ch-3 sp on **new Strip**; repeat from ★ 86 times **more**, ch 5, (sc
in next ch-3 sp, ch 5) 3 times; join with slip st to first sc,
finish off.

EDGING
With **right** side facing and working across short end of Afghan,
join yarn with slip st in ch-5 sp to right of first joining sc; ch 4,
† decrease, ch 1, dc in same sp, [ch 1, (dc, work Picot, dc,
ch 1) in each of next 4 ch-5 sps, dc in next ch-5 sp, ch 1,
decrease, ch 1, dc in same sp] 8 times, ch 1, (dc, work Picot,
dc, ch 1) in each of next 5 ch-5 sps, work Picot, (hdc in next
ch-5 sp, work Picot) 87 times, (dc, work Picot, dc, ch 1) in
each of next 5 ch-5 sps †, dc in next ch-5 sp, ch 1, repeat from
† to † once; join with slip st to third ch of beginning ch-4,
finish off.

ROCK-A-BYE PLAID

Horizontal and vertical stripes give this sport weight baby afghan the classic look of windowpane plaid. The stripes are simply slip stitched on after the afghan is finished.

Finished Size: 33" x 45"

MATERIALS
  Sport Weight Yarn:
    White - 15 ounces, (430 grams, 1,595 yards)
    Blue - 2 ounces, (60 grams, 215 yards)
  Crochet hook, size H (5.00 mm) **or** size needed
    for gauge

GAUGE: In pattern, 13 sts = 3¹/₂"; 10 rows = 3"

Gauge Swatch: 3¹/₂"w x 3"h
Ch 14 **loosely**.
Row 1 (Right side): Sc in second ch from hook and in each ch across: 13 sc.
Rows 2-10: Work same as Afghan.
Finish off.

AFGHAN BODY

With White, ch 118 **loosely**.
Row 1 (Right side): Sc in second ch from hook and in next 16 chs, ★ place marker around last sc made for Stripe placement, sc in next 4 chs, place marker around last sc made for Stripe placement, sc in next 16 chs; repeat from ★ across: 117 sc.
Note: Loop a short piece of yarn around any stitch to mark Row 1 as **right** side.
Row 2: Ch 1, turn; sc in first sc, ★ skip next sc, 3 dc in next sc, skip next sc, sc in next sc; repeat from ★ across.
Row 3: Ch 1, turn; sc in each st across.
Rows 4-140: Repeat Rows 2 and 3, 68 times; then repeat Row 2 once **more**.
Row 141: Ch 1, turn; sc in first 17 sts, ★ place marker around last sc made for Stripe placement, sc in next 4 sts, place marker around last sc made for Stripe placement, sc in next 16 sts; repeat from ★ across; finish off.

HORIZONTAL STRIPES

Note: Keep working yarn on **wrong** side of Afghan.
First Stripe: With **right** side facing and working in sc on Row 15, join Blue with slip st in first sc; slip st **loosely** in each sc across; finish off.

Second Stripe: With **right** side facing, counting up from last Stripe made, skip next 3 rows and join Blue with slip st in first sc of next row; slip st **loosely** in each sc across; finish off.
Third Stripe: With **right** side facing, counting up from last Stripe made, skip next 13 rows and join Blue with slip st in first sc of next row; slip st **loosely** in each sc across; finish off.
Repeat Second Stripe and Third Stripe, 5 times; then repeat Second Stripe once **more**.

VERTICAL STRIPES

Note: Keep working yarn on **wrong** side of Afghan.
First Stripe: With **right** side facing, join Blue with slip st in first marked sc on Row 1; working vertically across top of sc, slip st **loosely** in sc on each row across to corresponding marked sc on Row 141; finish off.
Remaining 9 Stripes: With **right** side facing, join Blue with slip st in next marked sc on Row 1; working vertically across top of sc, slip st **loosely** in sc on each row across to corresponding marked sc on Row 141; finish off.

EDGING

Rnd 1: With **right** side facing and working across sc on Row 141, join White with slip st in first sc; ch 1, 3 sc in same st, sc in each sc across to last sc, 3 sc in last sc; work 163 sc evenly spaced across end of rows; working in free loops of beginning ch *(Fig. 26b, page 142)*, 3 sc in first ch, sc in next 115 chs, 3 sc in next ch; work 163 sc evenly spaced across end of rows; join with slip st to first sc, finish off: 568 sc.
Rnd 2: With **right** side facing, join Blue with slip st in center sc of any corner 3-sc group; ch 1, 2 sc in same st, ★ sc in each sc across to center sc of next corner 3-sc group, 3 sc in center sc; repeat from ★ 2 times **more**, sc in each sc across, sc in same st as first sc; join with slip st to first sc: 576 sc.
Rnd 3: Ch 3, 4 dc in same st, skip next sc, sc in next sc, skip next sc, (3 dc in next sc, skip next sc, sc in next sc, skip next sc) across to center sc of next 3-sc group, ★ 5 dc in center sc, skip next sc, sc in next sc, skip next sc, (3 dc in next sc, skip next sc, sc in next sc, skip next sc) across to center sc of next 3-sc group; repeat from ★ 2 times **more**; join with slip st to top of beginning ch-3, finish off.

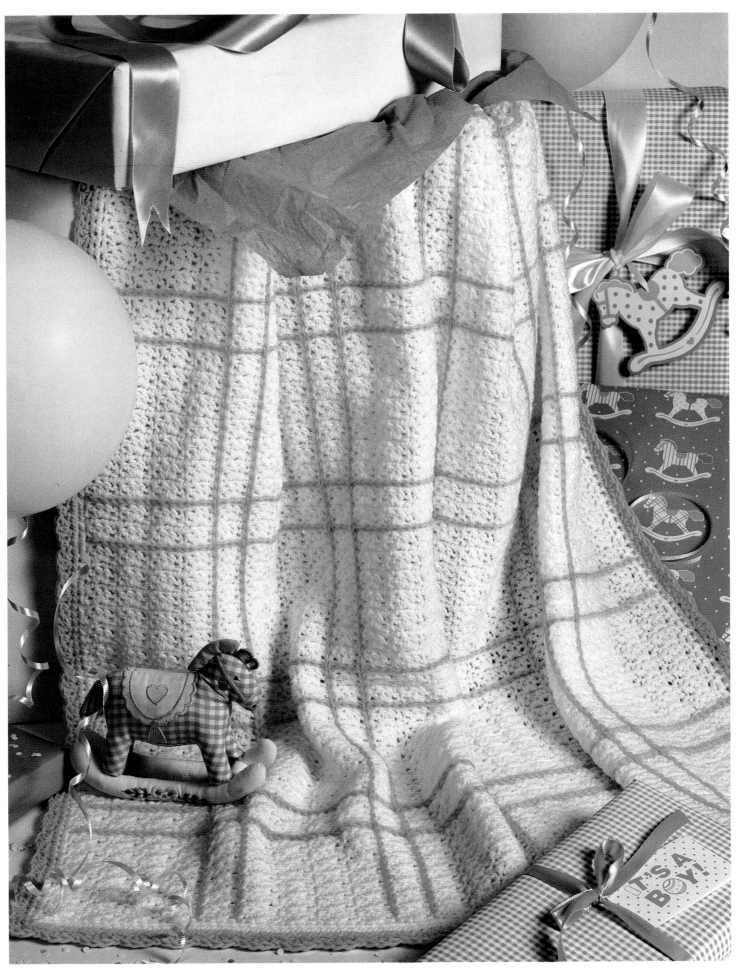

EMERALD ISLE MEDLEY

Bold and beautiful like the Emerald Isle, this handsome throw is a kaleidoscope of textures. Four shades of green yarn are woven with ecru to create the lush range of color, while clusters, long single crochets, and a medley of front post trebles form the pattern.

Finished Size: 48" x 63"

MATERIALS
Worsted Weight Yarn:
    Ecru - 40½ ounces, (1,150 grams, 2,790 yards)
    Very Lt Green - 7 ounces, (200 grams, 480 yards)
    Lt Green - 7 ounces, (200 grams, 480 yards)
    Green - 7 ounces, (200 grams, 480 yards)
    Dk Green - 7 ounces, (200 grams, 480 yards)
Crochet hook, size H (5.00 mm) **or** size needed
    for gauge

GAUGE: In pattern, 16 sts = 4½"; 24 rows = 5"

Gauge Swatch: 6"w x 5"h
Ch 22 **loosely**.
Work same as Afghan for 24 rows.
Finish off.

STITCH GUIDE

CLUSTER
★ YO, insert hook in sc indicated, YO and pull up a loop, YO and draw through 2 loops on hook; repeat from ★ 2 times **more**, YO and draw through all 4 loops on hook, ch 1 to close *(Fig. 15a, page 140)*.

LONG SINGLE CROCHET (abbreviated LSC)
Working **around** previous row, insert hook in sc one row **below** next sc, YO and pull up a loop even with loop on hook, YO and draw through both loops on hook *(Fig. 22, page 141)* **(counts as one sc)**.

FRONT POST DOUBLE TREBLE CROCHET (abbreviated FPdtr)
YO 3 times, insert hook from **front** to **back** around post of st indicated, YO and pull up a loop *(Fig. 13, page 139)*, (YO and draw through 2 loops on hook) 4 times. Skip sc behind FPdtr.

FRONT POST TREBLE CROCHET (abbreviated FPtr)
YO twice, insert hook from **front** to **back** around post of st indicated, YO and pull up a loop *(Fig. 12, page 139)*, (YO and draw through 2 loops on hook) 3 times. Skip sc behind FPtr.

COLOR SEQUENCE

4 Rows Ecru *(Fig. 27a, page 142)*, 1 row Lt Green, 2 rows Ecru, 1 row Very Lt Green, 3 rows Ecru, 1 row Dk Green, ★ 4 rows Ecru, 1 row Green, 2 rows Ecru, 1 row Lt Green, 3 rows Ecru, 1 row Very Lt Green, 4 rows Ecru, 1 row Dk Green, 2 rows Ecru, 1 row Green, 3 rows Ecru, 1 row Lt Green, 4 rows Ecru, 1 row Very Lt Green, 2 rows Ecru, 1 row Dk Green, 3 rows Ecru, 1 row Green, 4 rows Ecru, 1 row Lt Green, 2 rows Ecru, 1 row Very Lt Green, 3 rows Ecru, 1 row Dk Green; repeat from ★ 5 times **more**, then work 3 rows Ecru.

AFGHAN BODY

With Ecru, ch 170 **loosely**.
Row 1: Sc in second ch from hook and in each ch across: 169 sc.
Row 2 (Right side): Ch 1, turn; sc in each sc across.
Note: Loop a short piece of yarn around any stitch to mark Row 2 as **right** side.
Rows 3 and 4: Ch 1, turn; sc in each sc across.
Row 5: Ch 1, turn; sc in first 2 sc, work Cluster in next sc, (sc in next 3 sc, work Cluster in next sc) across to last 2 sc, sc in last 2 sc: 127 sc and 42 Clusters.
Row 6: Ch 1, turn; work 2 LSC, sc in next Cluster, (work 3 LSC, sc in next Cluster) across to last 2 sc, work 2 LSC: 169 sc.
Row 7: Ch 1, turn; sc in each sc across.
Row 8: Ch 1, turn; sc in first 4 sc, working 5 rows **below**, skip first 4 sc, work FPdtr around next sc, ★ sc in next 3 sc on **previous** row, working 5 rows **below**, skip next 3 sc from last FPdtr made, work FPdtr around next sc; repeat from ★ across to last 4 sc, sc in last 4 sc: 128 sc and 41 FPdtr.
Rows 9-11: Ch 1, turn; sc in each st across: 169 sc.
Row 12: Ch 1, turn; sc in first 3 sc, work FPtr around next FPdtr 4 rows **below**, sc in next sc on **previous** row, work FPtr around **same** st as last FPtr made, ★ sc in next sc on **previous** row, work FPtr around next FPdtr 4 rows **below**, sc in next sc on **previous** row, work FPtr around **same** st as last FPtr made; repeat from ★ across to last 3 sc, sc in last 3 sc: 87 sc and 82 FPtr.
Rows 13-16: Ch 1, turn; sc in each st across: 169 sc.
Rows 17-303: Repeat Rows 5-16, 23 times; then repeat Rows 5-15 once **more**.
Finish off.

EDGING
FIRST SIDE
With **right** side facing and working in end of rows, join Ecru with sc in first row *(see Joining With Sc, page 142)*; sc evenly across; finish off.

SECOND SIDE
With **right** side facing and working in end of rows, join Ecru with sc in first row; sc evenly across; finish off.

GRANNY'S LILACS

Abloom with lilacs, this lacy granny makes a lovely addition to the bedroom. Worked in squares of worsted weight yarn, the floral beauty captures the charm of the old-fashioned flowers.

Finished Size: 50" x 68"

MATERIALS
Worsted Weight Yarn:
  Ecru - 25½ ounces, (720 grams, 1,615 yards)
  Purple - 18½ ounces, (530 grams, 1,170 yards)
  Green - 15½ ounces, (440 grams, 980 yards)
Crochet hook, size I (5.50 mm) **or** size needed
  for gauge
Yarn needle

GAUGE: Each Square = 6"

Gauge Swatch: 3¾" in diameter
Work same as Square through Rnd 2.

STITCH GUIDE

> **DECREASE** (uses next 4 dc)
> † YO, insert hook in **next** dc, YO and pull up a loop, YO and draw through 2 loops on hook †, skip next 2 dc, repeat from † to † once, YO and draw through all 3 loops on hook **(counts as one dc)**.

SQUARE (Make 88)
With Purple, ch 10; join with slip st to form a ring.
Rnd 1 (Right side): Ch 3 **(counts as first dc, now and throughout)**, 2 dc in ring, ch 1, (3 dc in ring, ch 1) 7 times; join with slip st to first dc, finish off: 8 ch-1 sps.
Note: Loop a short piece of yarn around any stitch to mark Rnd 1 as **right** side.
Rnd 2: With **right** side facing, join Ecru with slip st in any ch-1 sp; ch 1, sc in same sp, ch 7, (sc in next ch-1 sp, ch 7) around; join with slip st to first sc, finish off: 8 ch-7 sps.
Rnd 3: With **right** side facing, join Green with slip st in center ch of any ch-7; ch 3, 6 dc in same st, 7 dc in center ch of next ch-7 and each ch-7 around; join with slip st to first dc, finish off: 56 dc.

Rnd 4: With **right** side facing and working in Back Loops Only **(Fig. 25, page 142)**, join Ecru with slip st in center dc of any 7-dc group; ch 1, sc in same st, ch 3, skip next dc, decrease, ch 3, skip next dc, tr in next dc, (ch 2, tr in same st) twice, ch 3, skip next dc, decrease, ch 3, skip next dc, ★ sc in next dc, ch 3, skip next dc, decrease, ch 3, skip next dc, tr in next dc, (ch 2, tr in same st) twice, ch 3, skip next dc, decrease, ch 3, skip next dc; repeat from ★ 2 times **more**; join with slip st to **both** loops of first sc: 24 sts and 24 sps.
Rnd 5: Ch 1, working in both loops, sc in same st, (3 sc in next ch-3 sp, sc in next st) twice, 2 sc in next ch-2 sp, (sc, ch 1, sc) in next tr, 2 sc in next ch-2 sp, ★ sc in next tr, (3 sc in next ch-3 sp, sc in next st) 4 times, 2 sc in next ch-2 sp, (sc, ch 1, sc) in next tr, 2 sc in next ch-2 sp; repeat from ★ 2 times **more**, (sc in next st, 3 sc in next ch-3 sp) twice; join with slip st to first sc, finish off: 92 sc and 4 ch-1 sps.
Rnd 6: With **right** side facing, join Purple with slip st in any corner ch-1 sp; ch 1, (sc in same sp, ch 1) twice, skip next sc, (sc in next sc, ch 1, skip next sc) across to next corner ch-1 sp, ★ (sc, ch 1) twice in ch-1 sp, skip next sc, (sc in next sc, ch 1, skip next sc) across to next corner ch-1 sp; repeat from ★ around; join with slip st to first sc, finish off: 52 sc and 52 ch-1 sps.

ASSEMBLY
With Purple and working through both loops, whipstitch Squares together **(Fig. 30b, page 143)**, forming 8 vertical strips of 11 Squares each, beginning in ch-1 sp of first corner and ending in ch-1 sp of next corner; whipstitch strips together in same manner.

EDGING

Rnd 1: With **right** side facing, join Purple with slip st in top right corner ch-1 sp; ch 1, (sc, ch 3, sc) in same sp, ch 1, (sc in next ch-1 sp, ch 1) 12 times, † sc in next joining, ch 1, (sc in next ch-1 sp, ch 1) 12 times †, repeat from † to † across to next corner ch-1 sp, ★ (sc, ch 3, sc) in ch-1 sp, ch 1, (sc in next ch-1 sp, ch 1) 12 times, repeat from † to † across to next corner ch-1 sp; repeat from ★ 2 times **more**; join with slip st to first sc, finish off: 494 ch-1 sps and 4 ch-3 sps.

Rnd 2: With **right** side facing, join Green with slip st in top right corner ch-3 sp; ch 3, 10 dc in same sp, † skip next ch-1 sp, sc in next ch-1 sp, skip next ch-1 sp, 7 dc in next ch-1 sp, skip next 2 ch-1 sps, sc in next ch-1 sp, (skip next ch-1 sp, 7 dc in next ch-1 sp, skip next ch-1 sp, sc in next ch-1 sp) across to within one ch-1 sp of next corner ch-3 sp, skip next ch-1 sp, 11 dc in ch-3 sp, skip next ch-1 sp, sc in next ch-1 sp, skip next ch-1 sp, (7 dc in next ch-1 sp, skip next ch-1 sp, sc in next ch-1 sp, skip next ch-1 sp) across to next corner ch-3 sp †, 11 dc in ch-3 sp, repeat from † to † once; join with slip st to first dc, finish off.

RAINBOW RIPPLE

The multicolored ripples in this throw resemble a sun-kissed rainbow! Seven soft shades of worsted weight yarn are worked in double crochet, V-stitches, and decreases to create the effect.

STITCH GUIDE

DECREASE (uses next 2 sts or sps)
★ YO, insert hook in **next** st or sp, YO and pull up a loop, YO and draw through 2 loops on hook; repeat from ★ once **more**, YO and draw through all 3 loops on hook (**counts as one dc**).
V-STITCH *(abbreviated V-St)*
(Dc, ch 1, dc) in next st.

COLOR SEQUENCE

3 Rows Pink *(Fig. 27a, page 142)*, one row White, ★ 3 rows Peach, one row White, 3 rows Yellow, one row White, 3 rows Green, one row White, 3 rows Blue, one row White, 3 rows Lavender, one row White, 3 rows Pink, one row White; repeat from ★ 3 times **more**.

Finished Size: 47" x 64"

MATERIALS
Worsted Weight Yarn:
Pink - 6 ounces,
(170 grams, 395 yards)
White - 6 ounces,
(170 grams, 395 yards)
Peach - 5 ounces,
(140 grams, 330 yards)
Yellow - 5 ounces,
(140 grams, 330 yards)
Green - 5 ounces,
(140 grams, 330 yards)
Blue - 5 ounces,
(140 grams, 330 yards)
Lavender - 5 ounces,
(140 grams, 330 yards)
Crochet hook, size I (5.50 mm) **or** size needed for gauge

GAUGE: Each repeat from point to point = 5¼"; 7 rows = 4½"

Gauge Swatch: 10½"w x 4½"h
Ch 51 **loosely.**
Work same as Afghan for 7 rows.
Finish off.

AFGHAN BODY

With Pink, ch 219 **loosely.**
Row 1 (Right side)**:** 2 Dc in fourth ch from hook (**3 skipped chs count as first dc**), dc in next 8 chs, decrease, skip next 2 chs, decrease, dc in next 8 chs, ★ work V-St twice, dc in next 8 chs, decrease, skip next 2 chs, decrease, dc in next 8 chs; repeat from ★ across to last ch, 3 dc in last ch: 200 dc and 16 ch-1 sps.
Note: Loop a short piece of yarn around any stitch to mark Row 1 as **right** side.
Rows 2 and 3: Ch 3 (**counts as first dc, now and throughout**), turn; 2 dc in same st, dc in next 8 dc, decrease, skip next 2 dc, decrease, ★ dc in next 7 dc and in next ch-1 sp, work V-St twice, dc in next ch-1 sp and in next 7 dc, decrease, skip next 2 dc, decrease; repeat from ★ across to last 9 dc, dc in next 8 dc, 3 dc in last dc changing to White in last dc.

Continued on page 53.

CURLY CUTIE

This little cutie is a delightful combination of twirls and curls! Fashioned in sport weight yarn, the cheery blanket will make a sweet addition to baby's room.

Finished Size: 37" x 46"

MATERIALS
Sport Weight Yarn:
    White - 18½ ounces, (530 grams, 1,480 yards)
    Green - 4 ounces, (110 grams, 320 yards)
    Yellow - 4 ounces, (110 grams, 320 yards)
    Pink - 4 ounces, (110 grams, 320 yards)
    Blue - 4 ounces, (110 grams, 320 yards)
Crochet hook, size G (4.00 mm) **or** size needed
    for gauge

GAUGE: In pattern, 12 sts and 8 rows = 3"

Gauge Swatch: 3¾"w x 3"h
Ch 17 **loosely**.
Work same as Afghan for 8 rows, omitting beginning and ending Twirls.

Note: Each row is worked across length of Afghan.

STITCH GUIDE

BEGINNING TWIRL
Ch 15 **loosely**, working under top loop and back ridge of chs *(Fig. 2c, page 137)*, 3 sc in second ch from hook and in each ch across.

ENDING TWIRL
Ch 15 **loosely**, working under top loop and back ridge of chs, 3 sc in second ch from hook and in each ch across, slip st in top of last sc made before ending Twirl.

CURL
Ch 3, working under top loop and back ridge of ch, 6 sc in second ch from hook.

AFGHAN BODY

With White, ch 185 **loosely**, place marker in third ch from hook for st placement.

Row 1 (Right side)**:** Dc in fourth ch from hook **(3 skipped chs count as first dc)** and in each ch across; finish off: 183 dc.

Note: Loop a short piece of yarn around any stitch to mark Row 1 as **right** side.

Row 2: With Green, work beginning Twirl; with **wrong** side of Afghan facing, sc in first dc, ch 1, skip next st, sc in next dc, work Curl, skip next st, sc in next dc, ★ (ch 1, skip next st, sc in next dc) 3 times, work Curl, skip next st, sc in next dc; repeat from ★ across to last 2 sts, ch 1, skip next st, sc in last dc, work ending Twirl; finish off: 23 Curls and 92 sc.

Row 3: With **right** side facing, join White with slip st in first sc (same st as slip st); ch 3 **(counts as first dc, now and throughout)**, working in **front** of next ch-1, tr in skipped st one row **below** ch-1, dc in next sc, working **behind** next Curl, tr in skipped st one row **below** Curl, dc in next sc, ★ (working in **front** of next ch-1, tr in skipped st one row **below** ch-1, dc in next sc) 3 times, working **behind** next Curl, tr in skipped st one row **below** Curl, dc in next sc; repeat from ★ across to last ch-1, working in **front** of last ch-1, tr in skipped st one row **below** ch-1, dc in last sc; finish off: 183 sts.

Row 4: With Yellow, work beginning Twirl; with **wrong** side of Afghan facing, sc in first dc, (ch 1, skip next tr, sc in next dc) 3 times, ★ work Curl, skip next tr, sc in next dc, (ch 1, skip next tr, sc in next dc) 3 times; repeat from ★ across, work ending Twirl; finish off: 22 Curls and 92 sc.

Row 5: With **right** side facing, join White with slip st in first sc (same st as slip st); ch 3, (working in **front** of next ch-1, tr in skipped tr one row **below** ch-1, dc in next sc) 3 times, ★ working **behind** next Curl, tr in skipped tr one row **below** Curl, dc in next sc, (working in **front** of next ch-1, tr in skipped tr one row **below** ch-1, dc in next sc) 3 times; repeat from ★ across; finish off: 183 sts.

Row 6: With Pink, repeat Row 2.

Row 7: Repeat Row 3.

Row 8: With Blue, repeat Row 4.

Row 9: Repeat Row 5.

Rows 10-97: Repeat Rows 2-9, 11 times.

Continued on page 52.

ROMANTIC DIAMONDS

The diamond-shaped "flowers" on this romantic wrap are decidedly feminine! The motifs are stitched in varying shades and pieced together with soft ecru motifs to complete the charming coverlet.

Finished Size: 49" x 58"

MATERIALS

Worsted Weight Yarn:
  Ecru - 15½ ounces, (440 grams, 1,065 yards)
  Green - 6 ounces, (170 grams, 410 yards)
  Lt Green - 4 ounces, (110 grams, 275 yards)
  Blue - 3 ounces, (90 grams, 205 yards)
  Purple - 3 ounces, (90 grams, 205 yards)
  Rose - 3 ounces, (90 grams, 205 yards)
  Navy - 3 ounces, (90 grams, 205 yards)
  Pink - 3 ounces, (90 grams, 205 yards)
  Teal - 3 ounces, (90 grams, 205 yards)
  Yellow - 2 ounces, (60 grams, 135 yards)
  Lt Blue - 2 ounces, (60 grams, 135 yards)
  Lt Purple - 2 ounces, (60 grams, 135 yards)
  Lt Rose - 2 ounces, (60 grams, 135 yards)
  Lt Navy - 2 ounces, (60 grams, 135 yards)
  Lt Pink - 2 ounces, (60 grams, 135 yards)
  Lt Teal - 2 ounces, (60 grams, 135 yards)
Crochet hook, size G (4.00 mm) **or** size needed
  for gauge

GAUGE SWATCH: Each Motif = 2½"
  (straight edge to straight edge)
Work same as First Motif.

FIRST MOTIF

With Ecru, ch 5; join with slip st to form a ring.
Rnd 1 (Right side)**:** Ch 1, 12 sc in ring; join with slip st to first sc: 12 sc.
Note: Loop a short piece of yarn around any stitch to mark Rnd 1 as **right** side.
Rnd 2: Ch 1, sc in same st, ch 3, skip next sc, (sc in next sc, ch 3, skip next sc) around; join with slip st to first sc: 6 ch-3 sps.
Rnd 3: Slip st in first ch-3 sp, ch 3 **(counts as first dc, now and throughout)**, (2 dc, ch 2, 3 dc) in same sp, (3 dc, ch 2, 3 dc) in each ch-3 sp around; join with slip st to first dc, finish off: 6 ch-2 sps.

ADDITIONAL MOTIFS

Following Placement Diagram, page 52, make Motifs using color indicated.
Ch 5; join with slip st to form a ring.
Rnds 1 and 2: Work same as First Motif: 6 ch-3 sps.
Note: When working joining, always insert hook from **back** to **front**.
Rnd 3 (Joining rnd)**:** Work One, Two, or Three Side Joining.

ONE SIDE JOINING

Rnd 3 (Joining rnd)**:** Slip st in first ch-3 sp, ch 3, (2 dc, ch 2, 3 dc) in same sp, (3 dc, ch 2, 3 dc) in next 3 ch-3 sps, 3 dc in next ch-3 sp, ch 1, drop loop from hook, holding Motifs with **wrong** sides together, insert hook in corresponding ch-2 sp on **adjacent Motif**, hook dropped loop and pull through *(Fig. 29, page 142)*, ch 1, 3 dc in same sp on **new Motif** and in next ch-3 sp, ch 1, drop loop from hook, insert hook in next ch-2 sp on **adjacent Motif**, hook dropped loop and pull through, ch 1, 3 dc in same sp on **new Motif**; join with slip st to first dc, finish off.

TWO SIDE JOINING

Rnd 3 (Joining rnd)**:** Slip st in first ch-3 sp, ch 3, (2 dc, ch 2, 3 dc) in same sp, (3 dc, ch 2, 3 dc) in next 2 ch-3 sps, 3 dc in next ch-3 sp, ch 1, drop loop from hook, holding Motifs with **wrong** sides together, insert hook in first unworked ch-2 sp to right of joining on **adjacent Motif**, hook dropped loop and pull through, ch 1, 3 dc in same sp on **new Motif** and in next ch-3 sp, drop loop from hook, insert hook in same sp as next joining on **adjacent Motif**, hook dropped loop and pull through, ch 1, 3 dc in same sp on **new Motif** and in next ch-3 sp, ch 1, drop loop from hook, insert hook in next unworked ch-2 sp on **adjacent Motif**, hook dropped loop and pull through, ch 1, 3 dc in same sp on **new Motif**; join with slip st to first dc, finish off.

Continued on page 52.

SPRING PANSIES

*Striking when worked in shades of a single hue, blue pansies
"bloom" on this springtime blanket. The floral motifs are whipstitched
to solid motifs to resemble a lovely latticework of flowers.*

Finished Size: 45" x 59"

MATERIALS

Worsted Weight Yarn:
- White - 40 ounces, (1,140 grams, 2,745 yards)
- Lt Blue - 3 ounces, (90 grams, 205 yards)
- Blue - 3 ounces, (90 grams, 205 yards)
- Dk Blue - 3 ounces, (90 grams, 205 yards)
- Black - 2 ounces, (60 grams, 135 yards)
- Gold - 3/4 ounce, (20 grams, 50 yards)

Crochet hook, size H (5.00 mm) **or** size needed
  for gauge

Yarn needle

GAUGE SWATCH: Each Motif = 3"
Work same as Solid Motif.

STITCH GUIDE

LONG SINGLE CROCHET (abbreviated LSC)
Insert hook from front to back **around** center ring **between**
second and third 3-dc groups, YO and pull up a loop, YO and
draw through both loops on hook **(Fig. 1)**.

Fig. 1

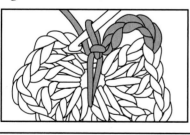

PANSY MOTIF (Make 54)

Note: The color used for Pansies, Rnds 2-4, varies. Make 18
Pansies with each of the following colors: Lt Blue, Blue, and Dk
Blue.

With Black, ch 4; join with slip st to form a ring.
Rnd 1 (Right side): Ch 3 **(counts as first dc, now and
throughout)**, 2 dc in ring, (ch 3, 3 dc in ring) 3 times
changing to Gold in last dc **(Fig. 27a, page 142)**, ch 5, work
LSC, ch 5; join with slip st to first dc, finish off: 3 ch-3 sps and
2 ch-5 sps.

Note: Loop a short piece of yarn around any stitch to mark
Rnd 1 as **right** side.

Rnd 2: With **right** side facing, join Pansy color with slip st in
second ch-5 sp to right of joining; ch 1, in same sp work [sc,
ch 3, hdc, ch 1, (dc, ch 1) 5 times, hdc, ch 3, sc] **(large Petal
made)**, sc in next LSC, work large Petal in next ch-5 sp, skip
next dc, sc in next dc, ★ (3 dc, ch 1, 3 dc) in next ch-3 sp
(small Petal made), skip next dc, sc in next dc; repeat from
★ 2 times **more**; join with slip st to first sc.

Rnd 3: Ch 3, (sc in next sp, ch 3) 8 times, skip next sc, sc in
next sc, ch 3, (sc in next sp, ch 3) 8 times, skip next sc, slip st
in next sc, leave 3 small Petals unworked.

Rnd 4: Ch 4, working **behind** Petals, (sc in next sc **between**
Petals, ch 4) 3 times, (slip st in center dc on Rnd 2 of next large
Petal, ch 4) twice; join with slip st to next slip st on Rnd 3, finish
off: 6 ch-4 sps.

Rnd 5: With **right** side facing, join White with sc in first ch-4 sp
(see Joining With Sc, page 142); 5 sc in same sp, 6 sc in
each ch-4 sp around; join with slip st to first sc: 36 sc.

Rnd 6: Ch 4, hdc in same st and in next 2 sc, sc in next 4 sc,
hdc in next 2 sc, ★ (hdc, ch 2, hdc) in next sc, hdc in next 2 sc,
sc in next 4 sc, hdc in next 2 sc; repeat from ★ 2 times **more**;
join with slip st to second ch of beginning ch-4, finish off: 40 sts
and 4 ch-2 sps.

SOLID MOTIF (Make 193)

With White, ch 5; join with slip st to form a ring.
Rnd 1 (Right side): Ch 6 **(counts as first dc plus ch 3)**,
(3 dc in ring, ch 3) 3 times, 2 dc in ring; join with slip st to first
dc: 4 ch-3 sps.

Note: Mark Rnd 1 as **right** side.

Rnd 2: Slip st in first ch-3 sp, ch 5 **(counts as first dc plus
ch 2, now and throughout)**, dc in same sp, ch 1, skip next
dc, (hdc, ch 1) twice in next dc, ★ (dc, ch 2, dc) in next
ch-3 sp, ch 1, skip next dc, (hdc, ch 1) twice in next dc; repeat
from ★ 2 times **more**; join with slip st to first dc: 16 sps.

Rnd 3: Slip st in first ch-2 sp, ch 5, 2 dc in same sp and in
each of next 3 ch-1 sps, ★ (2 dc, ch 2, 2 dc) in next ch-2 sp,
2 dc in each of next 3 ch-1 sps; repeat from ★ 2 times **more**,
dc in same sp as first dc; join with slip st to first dc, finish off:
40 dc and 4 ch-2 sps.

46

Continued on page 53.

ANGELS IN THE CLOUDS

This glorious afghan was inspired by the heavens above!
Worked in squares, it features lovely openwork shapes that
symbolize beautiful winged angels and fluffy clouds.

Finished Size: 47" x 62"

MATERIALS
Worsted Weight Yarn:
   47 ounces, (1,330 grams, 2,740 yards)
Crochet hook, size G (4.00 mm) **or** size needed
   for gauge

GAUGE: Each Square = 15"

Gauge Swatch: 3³/₄"
Work same as Cloud Square, page 50, through Rnd 3.

ANGEL SQUARE (Make 6)
Ch 6; join with slip st to form a ring.
Rnd 1 (Right side)**:** Ch 3 **(counts as first dc, now and throughout)**, 2 dc in ring, (ch 3, 3 dc in ring) 3 times, ch 1, hdc in first dc to form last ch-3 sp: 12 dc and 4 ch-3 sps.
Note: Loop a short piece of yarn around any stitch to mark Rnd 1 as **right** side.
Rnd 2: Ch 3, dc in same sp and in next 3 dc, ★ (2 dc, ch 3, 2 dc) in next ch-3 sp, dc in next 3 dc; repeat from ★ 2 times **more**, 2 dc in same sp as first dc, ch 1, hdc in first dc to form last ch-3 sp: 28 dc and 4 ch-3 sps.
Rnd 3: Ch 3, dc in same sp and in next 7 dc, (2 dc, ch 3, 2 dc) in next ch-3 sp, † dc in next 2 dc, ch 3, skip next 3 dc, dc in next 2 dc †, (2 dc, ch 3, 2 dc) in next ch-3 sp, dc in next dc, (ch 2, skip next 2 dc, dc in next dc) twice, (2 dc, ch 3, 2 dc) in next ch-3 sp, repeat from † to † once, 2 dc in same sp as first dc, ch 1, hdc in first dc to form last ch-3 sp: 34 dc and 8 sps.
Rnd 4: Ch 3, dc in same sp and in next dc, (ch 1, skip next dc, dc in next dc) 5 times, † (2 dc, ch 3, 2 dc) in next ch-3 sp, dc in next dc, ch 2, (dc, ch 5, dc) in next ch-3 sp, ch 2, skip next 3 dc, dc in next dc †, (2 dc, ch 3, 2 dc) in next ch-3 sp, ch 2, skip next 2 dc, dc in next dc, 5 dc in next dc, dc in next dc, ch 2, skip next 2 dc, repeat from † to † once, 2 dc in same sp as first dc, ch 1, hdc in first dc to form last ch-3 sp: 37 dc and 4 ch-3 sps.

Rnd 5: Ch 3, dc in same sp and in each dc and each ch-1 sp across to next ch-3 sp, † (2 dc, ch 3, 2 dc) in ch-3 sp, dc in next 3 dc, ch 3, skip next ch-2 sp, 2 sc in next ch-5 sp, ch 3, skip next ch-2 sp, dc in next 3 dc †, (2 dc, ch 3, 2 dc) in next ch-3 sp, dc in next 2 dc, 5 dc in next dc, skip next 2 dc, dc in next dc, skip next 2 dc, 5 dc in next dc, dc in next 2 dc, repeat from † to † once, 2 dc in same sp as first dc, ch 1, hdc in first dc to form last ch-3 sp: 58 dc and 8 ch-3 sps.
Rnd 6: Ch 3, dc in same sp and in next dc, ★ ch 1, skip next dc, dc in next dc; repeat from ★ across to next ch-3 sp, † (2 dc, ch 3, 2 dc) in ch-3 sp, dc in next 2 dc, ch 6, sc in next ch-3 sp, sc in next 2 sc and in next ch-3 sp, ch 6, skip next 3 dc, dc in next 2 dc †, (2 dc, ch 3, 2 dc) in next ch-3 sp, dc in next 4 dc, ch 2, skip next 2 dc, dc in next dc, skip next 2 dc, 5 dc in next dc, skip next 2 dc, dc in next dc, ch 2, skip next 2 dc, dc in next 4 dc, repeat from † to † once, 2 dc in same sp as first dc, ch 1, hdc in first dc to form last ch-3 sp: 49 dc, 8 sc, and 4 ch-3 sps.
Rnd 7: Ch 3, dc in same sp and in each dc and each ch-1 sp across to next ch-3 sp, † (2 dc, ch 3, 2 dc) in ch-3 sp, dc in next 4 dc, ch 5, 2 sc in next ch-6 sp, sc in next 4 sc, 2 sc in next ch-6 sp, ch 5, dc in next 4 dc †, (2 dc, ch 3, 2 dc) in next ch-3 sp, dc in next 6 dc, 2 dc in next ch-2 sp, dc in next dc, (ch 2, skip next 2 dc, dc in next dc) twice, 2 dc in next ch-2 sp, dc in next 6 dc, repeat from † to † once, 2 dc in same sp as first dc, ch 1, hdc in first dc to form last ch-3 sp: 74 dc, 16 sc, and 4 ch-3 sps.
Rnd 8: Ch 3, dc in same sp and in next dc, ★ ch 1, skip next dc, dc in next dc; repeat from ★ across to next ch-3 sp, † (2 dc, ch 3, 2 dc) in ch-3 sp, dc in next 3 dc, ch 6, 3 sc in next ch-5 sp, sc in next 8 sc, 3 sc in next ch-5 sp, ch 6, skip next 3 dc, dc in next 3 dc †, (2 dc, ch 3, 2 dc) in next ch-3 sp, dc in next 11 dc, 2 dc in next ch-2 sp, dc in next dc, 2 dc in next ch-2 sp, dc in next 11 dc, repeat from † to † once, 2 dc in same sp as first dc, ch 1, hdc in first dc to form last ch-3 sp; do **not** finish off: 69 dc, 28 sc, and 4 ch-3 sps.

Continued on page 50.

48

Rnd 9: Ch 3, dc in same sp and in each dc and each ch-1 sp across to next ch-3 sp, † (2 dc, ch 3, 2 dc) in ch-3 sp, dc in next 5 dc, ch 6, sc in next 3 sc, ch 7, skip next 8 sc, sc in next 3 sc, ch 6, dc in next 5 dc †, (2 dc, ch 3, 2 dc) in next ch-3 sp, dc in each dc across to next ch-3 sp, repeat from † to † once, 2 dc in same sp as first dc, ch 1, hdc in first dc to form last ch-3 sp: 98 dc, 12 sc and 4 ch-3 sps.

Rnd 10: Ch 3, dc in same sp and in next dc, ★ ch 1, skip next dc, dc in next dc; repeat from ★ across to next ch-3 sp, † (2 dc, ch 3, 2 dc) in ch-3 sp, dc in next 7 dc, 3 dc in next ch-6 sp, ch 7, 8 sc in next ch-7 sp, ch 7, 3 dc in next ch-6 sp, dc in next 7 dc †, (2 dc, ch 3, 2 dc) in next ch-3 sp, dc in each dc across to next ch-3 sp, repeat from † to † once, 2 dc in same sp as first dc, ch 1, hdc in first dc to form last ch-3 sp: 109 dc, 16 sc, and 4 ch-3 sps.

Rnd 11: Ch 3, dc in same sp and in next 3 dc, ch 1, (dc in next dc, ch 1) 16 times, dc in next 3 dc, † (2 dc, ch 3, 2 dc) in next ch-3 sp, dc in next 12 dc, 3 dc in next ch-7 sp, ch 7, skip next 3 sc, sc in next 2 sc, ch 7, 3 dc in next ch-7 sp, dc in next 12 dc †, (2 dc, ch 3, 2 dc) in next ch-3 sp, dc in each dc across to next ch-3 sp, repeat from † to † once, 2 dc in same sp as first dc, ch 1, hdc in first dc to form last ch-3 sp: 137 dc and 4 ch-3 sps.

Rnd 12: Ch 3, dc in same sp and in each dc and each ch-1 sp across to next ch-3 sp, † (2 dc, ch 3, 2 dc) in ch-3 sp, dc in next 17 dc, 3 dc in next ch-7 sp, ch 2, 3 dc in next ch-7 sp, dc in next 17 dc †, (2 dc, ch 3, 2 dc) in next ch-3 sp, dc in each dc across to next ch-3 sp, repeat from † to † once, 2 dc in same sp as first dc, ch 1, hdc in first dc to form last ch-3 sp: 182 dc and 4 ch-3 sps.

Rnd 13: Ch 3, dc in same sp and in each dc across to next ch-3 sp, † (2 dc, ch 3, 2 dc) in ch-3 sp, dc in next 22 dc, 3 dc in next ch-2 sp, dc in next 22 dc †, (2 dc, ch 3, 2 dc) in next ch-3 sp, dc in each dc across to next ch-3 sp, repeat from † to † once, 2 dc in same sp as first dc, ch 1, hdc in first dc to form last ch-3 sp: 204 dc and 4 ch-3 sps.

Rnd 14: Ch 4, dc in next dc, place marker around dc just made to mark bottom edge, ch 1, (skip next dc, dc in next dc, ch 1) across to next ch-3 sp, ★ (dc, ch 3, dc) in ch-3 sp, ch 1, dc in next dc, ch 1, (skip next dc, dc in next dc, ch 1) across to next ch-3 sp; repeat from ★ 2 times **more**, dc in same sp as first dc, ch 3; join with slip st to third ch of beginning ch-4, finish off: 112 sps.

CLOUD SQUARE (Make 6)

Ch 6; join with slip st to form a ring.

Rnd 1 (Right side)**:** Ch 3, 2 dc in ring, (ch 3, 3 dc in ring) 3 times, ch 1, hdc in first dc to form last ch-3 sp: 12 dc and 4 ch-3 sps.

Note: Mark Rnd 1 as **right** side.

Rnd 2: Ch 3, dc in same sp and in next 3 dc, ★ (2 dc, ch 3, 2 dc) in next ch-3 sp, dc in next 3 dc; repeat from ★ 2 times **more**, 2 dc in same sp as first dc, ch 1, hdc in first dc to form last ch-3 sp: 28 dc and 4 ch-3 sps.

Rnds 3 and 4: Ch 3, dc in same sp and in each dc across to next ch-3 sp, ★ (2 dc, ch 3, 2 dc) in ch-3 sp, dc in each dc across to next ch-3 sp; repeat from ★ 2 times **more**; 2 dc in same sp as first dc, ch 1, hdc in first dc to form last ch-3 sp: 60 dc and 4 ch-3 sps.

Rnd 5: Ch 3, dc in same sp and in next 5 dc, ch 2, skip next 2 dc, dc in next dc, ch 2, skip next 2 dc, dc in next 5 dc, ★ (2 dc, ch 3, 2 dc) in next ch-3 sp, dc in next 5 dc, ch 2, skip next 2 dc, dc in next dc, ch 2, skip next 2 dc, dc in next 5 dc; repeat from ★ 2 times **more**, 2 dc in same sp as first dc, ch 1, hdc in first dc to form last ch-3 sp: 60 dc and 12 sps.

Rnd 6: Ch 3, dc in same sp and in next 4 dc, ch 2, skip next 2 dc, dc in next dc, 5 dc in next dc, dc in next dc, ch 2, skip next 2 dc, dc in next 4 dc, ★ (2 dc, ch 3, 2 dc) in next ch-3 sp, dc in next 4 dc, ch 2, skip next 2 dc, dc in next dc, 5 dc in next dc, dc in next dc, ch 2, skip next 2 dc, dc in next 4 dc; repeat from ★ 2 times **more**, 2 dc in same sp as first dc, ch 1, hdc in first dc to form last ch-3 sp: 76 dc and 12 sps.

Rnd 7: Ch 3, dc in same sp and in next 3 dc, ch 2, skip next 2 dc, dc in next dc, 5 dc in next dc, skip next 2 dc, dc in next dc, skip next 2 dc, 5 dc in next dc, dc in next dc, ch 2, skip next 2 dc, dc in next 3 dc, ★ (2 dc, ch 3, 2 dc) in next ch-3 sp, dc in next 3 dc, ch 2, skip next 2 dc, dc in next dc, 5 dc in next dc, skip next 2 dc, dc in next dc, skip next 2 dc, 5 dc in next dc, dc in next dc, ch 2, skip next 2 dc, dc in next 3 dc; repeat from ★ 2 times **more**, 2 dc in same sp as first dc, ch 1, hdc in first dc to form last ch-3 sp: 92 dc and 12 sps.

RAINBOW RIPPLE Continued from page 40.

Row 4: Ch 1, turn; sc in first dc, ch 1, skip next dc, (sc in next dc, ch 1, skip next dc) 4 times, sc in next 4 dc, ★ ch 1, (skip next dc, sc in next dc, ch 1) 4 times, skip next ch, sc in next 2 dc, ch 1, (skip next st, sc in next dc, ch 1) 4 times, skip next dc, sc in next 4 dc; repeat from ★ across to last 10 dc, (ch 1, skip next dc, sc in next dc) 5 times: 126 sc and 90 ch-1 sps.

Row 5: Ch 3, turn; 2 dc in same st, (dc in next ch-1 sp and in next sc) 4 times, decrease, skip next 2 sc, decrease, (dc in next sc and in next ch-1 sp) 4 times, ★ work V-St twice, (dc in next ch-1 sp and in next sc) 4 times, decrease, skip next 2 sc, decrease, (dc in next sc and in next ch-1 sp) 4 times; repeat from ★ across to last sc, 3 dc in last sc: 200 dc and 16 ch-1 sps.

Rows 6 and 7: Ch 3, turn; 2 dc in same st, dc in next 8 dc, decrease, skip next 2 dc, decrease, ★ dc in next 7 dc and in next ch-1 sp, work V-St twice, dc in next ch-1 sp and in next 7 dc, decrease, skip next 2 dc, decrease; repeat from ★ across to last 9 dc, dc in next 8 dc, 3 dc in last dc.

Rows 8-100: Repeat Rows 4-7, 23 times; then repeat Row 4 once **more**.
Finish off.

BOTTOM EDGING

Row 1: With **wrong** side facing and working in free loops of beginning ch *(Fig. 26b, page 142)*, join White with slip st in first ch (at base of first 3 dc); ch 1, sc in same ch, ch 1, (skip next ch, sc in next ch, ch 1) 4 times, skip next ch, sc in next 2 chs, ch 1, sc in next 2 chs, ★ ch 1, (skip next ch, sc in next ch, ch 1) 3 times, skip next ch, sc in next 2 chs, skip next 2 chs, sc in next 2 chs, ch 1, (skip next ch, sc in next ch, ch 1) 3 times, skip next ch, sc in next 2 chs, ch 1, sc in next 2 chs; repeat from ★ across to last 10 chs, (ch 1, skip next ch, sc in next ch) 5 times; finish off.

SPRING PANSIES Continued from page 46.

ASSEMBLY

Hold each Pansy Motif with center small Petal at bottom edge. With White and using Placement Diagram as a guide, and working through both loops of each sc, whipstitch Squares together forming Strips *(Fig. 30b, page 143)*, beginning in second ch of first corner ch-2 and ending in first ch of next corner ch-2; whipstitch strips together in same manner.

PLACEMENT DIAGRAM

KEY
C - Lt Blue
D - Blue
E - Dk Blue

EDGING

Rnd 1: With **right** side facing, join White with sc in corner ch-2 sp at Point A on Placement Diagram; ch 5, sc in same sp, ch 3, skip next st, sc in next st, skip next 2 sts, (dc, ch 1) 3 times in next st, dc in next st, (ch 1, dc in same st) twice, skip next 2 sts, sc in next st, ch 3, † (sc, ch 5, sc) in next ch-2 sp, ch 3, skip next st, sc in next st, skip next 2 sts, (dc, ch 1) 3 times in next st, dc in next st, (ch 1, dc in same st) twice, skip next 2 sts, sc in next st and in next sp, skip joining, sc in next sp, skip next st, sc in next st, skip next 2 sts, (dc, ch 1) 3 times in next st, dc in next st, (ch 1, dc in same st) twice, skip next 2 sts, sc in next st, ch 3 †, repeat from † to † around to Point B, (sc, ch 5, sc) in next ch-2 sp, ch 3, skip next st, sc in next st, skip next 2 sts, (dc, ch 1) 3 times in next st, dc in next st, (ch 1, dc in same st) twice, skip next 2 sts, sc in next st, ch 3, repeat from † to † across; join with slip st to first sc.

Rnd 2: Slip st in first ch-5 sp, ch 1, (sc, ch 3, sc, ch 5, sc, ch 3, sc) in same sp, sc in next ch-3 sp, † (sc in next ch-1 sp, ch 3) twice, (sc, ch 5, sc) in next ch-1 sp, (ch 3, sc in next ch-1 sp) twice, sc in next ch-3 sp, (sc, ch 3, sc, ch 5, sc, ch 3, sc) in next ch-5 sp, sc in next ch-3 sp, (sc in next ch-1 sp, ch 3) twice, (sc, ch 5, sc) in next ch-1 sp, (ch 3, sc in next ch-1 sp) twice †, repeat from † to † around to Point C, sc in next ch-3 sp, (sc, ch 3, sc, ch 5, sc, ch 3, sc) in next ch-5 sp, sc in next ch-3 sp, (sc in next ch-1 sp, ch 3) twice, (sc, ch 5, sc) in next ch-1 sp, (ch 3, sc in next ch-1 sp) twice, repeat from † to † 8 times, (sc in next ch-1 sp, ch 3) twice, (sc, ch 5, sc) in next ch-1 sp, (ch 3, sc in next ch-1 sp) twice, sc in last ch-3 sp; join with slip st to first sc, finish off.

GARDEN STROLL

This lush throw is as delightful as strolling through a formal garden. Crocheted in strips, the wrap gets its lattice look from cross stitches and treble crochets.

Finished Size: 53" x 73"

MATERIALS
Worsted Weight Yarn:
Green - 40 ounces,
(1,140 grams, 2,630 yards)
Off-White - 21 ounces,
(600 grams, 1,380 yards)
Crochet hook, size H (5.00 mm) **or** size needed for gauge
Yarn needle

GAUGE: Each Strip = 5¹/4" wide

Gauge Swatch: 3¹/4"w x 4¹/4"h
Work same as Center through Row 6.
Finish off.

STITCH GUIDE

FRONT POST TREBLE CROCHET (abbreviated FPtr)
YO twice, insert hook from **front** to **back** around post of st indicated, YO and pull up a loop *(Fig. 12, page 139)*, (YO and draw through 2 loops on hook) 3 times. Skip st behind FPtr.
CROSS STITCH (uses next 2 dc)
(abbreviated Cross St)
Skip next dc, dc in next dc, working **around** dc just made, dc in skipped dc.

STRIP (Make 10)
CENTER
With Green, ch 18 **loosely**.
Row 1 (Right side)**:** Dc in seventh ch from hook, working **around** dc just made, dc in sixth skipped ch, ch 1, ★ skip next 2 chs, dc in next ch, working **around** dc just made, dc in second skipped ch, ch 1; repeat from ★ 2 times **more**, skip next ch, dc in last ch: 9 dc and 5 sps.
Note: Loop a short piece of yarn around any stitch to mark Row 1 as **right** side and bottom edge.
Row 2: Ch 4 **(counts as first dc plus ch 1, now and throughout)**, turn; (work Cross St, ch 1) 4 times, skip next ch, dc in next ch: 4 Cross Sts and 2 dc.
Rows 3-101: Ch 4, turn; (work Cross St, ch 1) 4 times, skip next ch, dc in last dc.
Finish off.

BORDER
Rnd 1: With **right** side facing and working in end of rows, join Off-White with slip st in Row 1; ch 3 **(counts as first dc)**, 5 dc in same row, 3 dc in next row and in each row across to last row, 6 dc in last row; working in sps across Row 101, 3 dc in each of next 3 ch-1 sps; working in end of rows, 6 dc in first row, 3 dc in next row and in each row across to last row, 6 dc in last row; working in sps across beginning ch, 3 dc in each of next 3 sps; join with slip st to first dc, finish off: 636 dc.

Continued on page 63.

TRANQUIL GRANNY

Crocheted in black, this granny square afghan is abloom with florals in a spectrum of tranquil purples, greens, and blues. The traditional throw is worked in squares that are simply whipstitched together.

Finished Size: 50" x 69"

MATERIALS

Worsted Weight Yarn:
- Black - 29 ounces, (820 grams, 1,990 yards)
- Lt Green - 4 ounces, (110 grams, 275 yards)
- Green - 4 ounces, (110 grams, 275 yards)
- Lt Purple - 4 ounces, (110 grams, 275 yards)
- Purple - 4 ounces, (110 grams, 275 yards)
- Lt Blue - 4 ounces, (110 grams, 275 yards)
- Blue - 4 ounces, (110 grams, 275 yards)

Crochet hook, size I (5.50 mm) **or** size needed for gauge

Yarn needle

GAUGE SWATCH: Each Square = 4³/₄"

SQUARE

Make 117 in the following color sequence.

	Square A Make 20	Square B Make 20	Square C Make 20
Rnd 1	Lt Blue	Green	Lt Purple
Rnd 2	Black	Black	Black
Rnd 3	Blue	Lt Green	Purple
Rnd 4	Black	Black	Black

	Square D Make 19	Square E Make 19	Square F Make 19
Rnd 1	Blue	Lt Green	Purple
Rnd 2	Black	Black	Black
Rnd 3	Lt Blue	Green	Lt Purple
Rnd 4	Black	Black	Black

Rnd 1 (Right side)**:** With color indicated, ch 4, 2 dc in fourth ch from hook, ch 3, (3 dc in same ch, ch 3) 3 times; join with slip st to top of beginning ch-4, finish off: 4 ch-3 sps.
Note: Loop a short piece of yarn around any stitch to mark Rnd 1 as **right** side.

Rnd 2: With **right** side facing, join Black with slip st in any ch-3 sp; ch 3 **(counts as first dc, now and throughout)**, (2 dc, ch 3, 3 dc) in same sp, ch 1, ★ (3 dc, ch 3, 3 dc) in next ch-3 sp, ch 1; repeat from ★ 2 times **more**; join with slip st to first dc, finish off: 24 dc and 8 sps.

Rnd 3: With **right** side facing, join next color with slip st in any corner ch-3 sp; ch 3, (2 dc, ch 3, 3 dc) in same sp, ch 1, 3 dc in next ch-1 sp, ch 1, ★ (3 dc, ch 3, 3 dc) in next corner ch-3 sp, ch 1, 3 dc in next ch-1 sp, ch 1; repeat from ★ 2 times **more**; join with slip st to first dc, finish off: 36 dc and 12 sps.

Rnd 4: With **right** side facing, join Black with slip st in any corner ch-3 sp; ch 3, (2 dc, ch 3, 3 dc) in same sp, ch 1, (3 dc in next ch-1 sp, ch 1) twice, ★ (3 dc, ch 3, 3 dc) in next corner ch-3 sp, ch 1, (3 dc in next ch-1 sp, ch 1) twice; repeat from ★ 2 times **more**; join with slip st to first dc, finish off: 48 dc and 16 sps.

ASSEMBLY

With Black, using Placement Diagram as a guide, and working through both loops, whipstitch Squares together **(Fig. 30b, page 143)**, forming 9 vertical strips of 13 Squares each, beginning in center ch of first corner ch-3 and ending in center ch of next corner ch-3; whipstitch strips together in same manner.

PLACEMENT DIAGRAM

A	B	C	D	E	F	A	B	C
F	A	B	C	D	E	F	A	B
E	F	A	B	C	D	E	F	A
D	E	F	A	B	C	D	E	F
C	D	E	F	A	B	C	D	E
B	C	D	E	F	A	B	C	D
A	B	C	D	E	F	A	B	C
F	A	B	C	D	E	F	A	B
E	F	A	B	C	D	E	F	A
D	E	F	A	B	C	D	E	F
C	D	E	F	A	B	C	D	E
B	C	D	E	F	A	B	C	D
A	B	C	D	E	F	A	B	C

56

Continued on page 64.

"PURR-FECTION!"

*This gem of an afghan is pure "purr-fection"! The squares
are arranged to form an intricate pattern of cluster diamonds,
and a chain of clusters composes the elegant border.*

Finished Size: 51" x 64"

MATERIALS

Worsted Weight Yarn:
  Ecru - 38 ounces, (1,080 grams, 2,605 yards)
  Green - 10 ounces,(280 grams, 685 yards)
  Rose - 9¹/₂ ounces, (270 grams, 650 yards)
Crochet hook, size I (5.50 mm) **or** size needed
  for gauge
Yarn needle

GAUGE: Each Square = 6¹/₂"

Gauge Swatch: 3"
Work same as Square through Rnd 3.

STITCH GUIDE

CLUSTER
Ch 3, YO, insert hook in third ch from hook, YO and pull
up a loop, YO and draw through 2 loops on hook, YO,
insert hook in same ch, YO and pull up a loop, YO and
draw through 2 loops on hook, YO and draw through all
3 loops on hook *(Fig. 15a, page 140)*.

CORNER CLUSTER
Ch 4, YO, insert hook in third ch from hook, YO and pull
up a loop, YO and draw through 2 loops on hook, YO,
insert hook in same ch, YO and pull up a loop, YO and
draw through 2 loops on hook, YO and draw through all
3 loops on hook, ch 1.

SQUARE (Make 63)

Rnd 1 (Right side)**:** With Ecru, ch 4, 2 dc in fourth ch from
hook **(3 skipped chs count as first dc)**, ch 3, (3 dc in
same ch, ch 3) 3 times; join with slip st to first dc, finish off:
12 dc and 4 ch-3 sps.
Note: Loop a short piece of yarn around any stitch to mark
Rnd 1 as **right** side.
Rnd 2: With **wrong** side facing, join Rose with sc in any
ch-3 sp *(see Joining With Sc, page 142)*; work Cluster,
sc in same sp, ch 3, ★ (sc, work Cluster, sc) in next ch-3 sp,
ch 3; repeat from ★ 2 times **more**; join with slip st to first
sc, finish off: 4 Clusters and 4 ch-3 sps.

Rnd 3: With **right** side facing, join Ecru with sc in first sc to left
of any Cluster; ★ † working in **front** of next ch-3, dc in next
3 dc one rnd **below** ch-3, sc in next sc, working **behind** next
Cluster, (dc, ch 3, dc) in sp **before** next sc one rnd **below**
Cluster *(Fig. 28, page 142)* †, sc in next sc; repeat from ★
2 times **more**, then repeat from † to † once; join with slip st to
first sc, finish off: 28 sts and 4 ch-3 sps.
Rnd 4: With **wrong** side facing, join Green with sc in any
corner ch-3 sp; work Cluster, sc in same sp, ★ † ch 3, skip next
3 sts, sc in next dc, ch 3, skip next 3 sts †, (sc, work Cluster, sc)
in next corner ch-3 sp; repeat from ★ 2 times **more**, then
repeat from † to † once; join with slip st to first sc, finish off:
12 sc and 8 ch-3 sps.
Rnd 5: With **right** side facing, join Ecru with sc in first sc to left
of any Cluster; ★ † (working in **front** of next ch-3, dc in next
3 sts one rnd **below** ch-3, sc in next sc) twice, working **behind**
next Cluster, (dc, ch 3, dc) in sp **before** next sc one rnd **below**
Cluster †, sc in next sc; repeat from ★ 2 times **more**, then
repeat from † to † once; join with slip st to first sc, finish off:
44 sts and 4 ch-3 sps.
Rnd 6: With **wrong** side facing, join Rose with sc in any corner
ch-3 sp; work Cluster, sc in same sp, ★ † ch 3, skip next 3 sts,
(sc in next dc, ch 3, skip next 3 sts) twice †, (sc, work Cluster,
sc) in next corner ch-3 sp; repeat from ★ 2 times **more**, then
repeat from † to † once; join with slip st to first sc, finish off:
16 sc and 12 ch-3 sps.
Rnd 7: With **right** side facing, join Ecru with sc in first sc to left
of any Cluster; ★ † (working in **front** of next ch-3, dc in next
3 sts one rnd **below** ch-3, sc in next sc) 3 times, working
behind next Cluster, (dc, ch 3, dc) in sp **before** next sc one
rnd **below** Cluster †, sc in next sc; repeat from ★ 2 times
more, then repeat from † to † once; join with slip st to first sc,
finish off: 60 sts and 4 ch-3 sps.
Rnd 8: With **wrong** side facing, join Green with sc in any
corner ch-3 sp; work Cluster, sc in same sp, ch 3, skip next
3 sts, (sc in next dc, ch 3, skip next 3 sts) 3 times, ★ (sc, work
Cluster, sc) in next corner ch-3 sp, ch 3, skip next 3 sts, (sc in
next dc, ch 3, skip next 3 sts) 3 times; repeat from ★ 2 times
more; join with slip st to first sc, finish off: 20 sc and
16 ch-3 sps.

Continued on page 65.

FLORAL SAMPLER

Romance abounds on this floral throw, which features a sampling of springtime flowers. Crocheted in pretty pastels, the afghan is a well-planned garden of colorful motifs.

Finished Size: 45" x 68"

MATERIALS
Worsted Weight Yarn:
- Ecru - 19 ounces, (540 grams, 1,305 yards)
- Green - 16 ounces, (450 grams, 1,095 yards)
- Lt Rose - 13 ounces, (370 grams, 890 yards)
- Navy - 2 ounces, (60 grams, 135 yards)
- Purple - 2 ounces, (60 grams, 135 yards)
- Yellow - 1½ ounces, (40 grams, 105 yards)
- Rose - 1 ounce, (30 grams, 70 yards)
Crochet hook, size G (4.00 mm) **or** size needed for gauge
Yarn needle

GAUGE: Each Motif = 6¾"
(straight edge to straight edge)

Gauge Swatches:
Motif A: Rnds 1-3 = 3½"
Motif B: Rnds 1 and 2 = 3"
Motif C: Rnd 1 = 1½"

STITCH GUIDE

2-DC CLUSTER
★ YO, insert hook in sp indicated, YO and pull up a loop, YO and draw through 2 loops on hook; repeat from ★ once **more**, YO and draw through all 3 loops on hook (*Fig. 15a, page 140*).

3-DC CLUSTER
★ YO, insert hook in sp indicated, YO and pull up a loop, YO and draw through 2 loops on hook; repeat from ★ 2 times **more**, YO and draw through all 4 loops on hook.

4-DC CLUSTER
★ YO, insert hook in sp indicated, YO and pull up a loop, YO and draw through 2 loops on hook; repeat from ★ 3 times **more**, YO and draw through all 5 loops on hook.

LONG HALF DOUBLE CROCHET (*abbreviated LHDC*)
YO, insert hook in ring and pull up a ½" loop, YO and draw through all 3 loops on hook.

DECREASE (uses next 2 sts)
★ YO, insert hook in **next** st, YO and pull up a loop, YO and draw through 2 loops on hook; repeat from ★ once **more**, YO and draw through all 3 loops on hook (**counts as one dc**).

REVERSE SINGLE CROCHET
(*abbreviated reverse sc*)
Working from **left** to **right**, insert hook in st to right of hook, YO and draw through, under, and to left of loop on hook (2 loops on hook), YO and draw through both loops on hook (**reverse sc made,** *Figs. 23a-d, page 141*).

MOTIF A (Make 25)

With Navy, ch 4; join with slip st to form a ring.

Rnd 1 (Right side)**:** Ch 1, 12 sc in ring; join with slip st to first sc: 12 sc.

Note: Loop a short piece of yarn around any stitch to mark Rnd 1 as **right** side.

Rnd 2: Ch 5 (**counts as first dc plus ch 2**), (dc in next sc, ch 2) around; join with slip st to first dc, finish off: 12 ch-2 sps.

Rnd 3: With **right** side facing, join Green with slip st in any ch-2 sp; ch 2, work 3-dc Cluster in same sp, ch 3, (work 4-dc Cluster in next ch-2 sp, ch 3) around; join with slip st to top of first 3-dc Cluster, finish off: 12 Clusters.

Rnd 4: With **right** side facing, join Ecru with slip st in any ch-3 sp; ch 3 (**counts as first dc, now and throughout**), 3 dc in same sp, ch 1, (4 dc in next ch-3 sp, ch 1) around; join with slip st to first dc, finish off: 12 ch-1 sps.

Rnd 5: With **right** side facing, join Lt Rose with slip st in any ch-1 sp; ch 3, (2 dc, ch 2, 3 dc) in same sp, ch 2, 4 dc in next ch-1 sp, ch 2, ★ (3 dc, ch 2, 3 dc) in next ch-1 sp, ch 2, 4 dc in next ch-1 sp, ch 2; repeat from ★ around; join with slip st to first dc: 18 ch-2 sps.

Rnd 6: Slip st in next 2 dc and in next ch-2 sp, ch 3, (2 dc, ch 2, 3 dc) in same sp, 4 dc in each of next 2 ch-2 sps, ★ (3 dc, ch 2, 3 dc) in next ch-2 sp, 4 dc in each of next 2 ch-2 sps; repeat from ★ around; join with slip st to first dc, finish off: 84 dc and 6 ch-2 sps.

Continued on page 62.

MOTIF B (Make 21)

With Yellow, ch 6; join with slip st to form a ring.

Rnd 1 (Right side): Ch 2, work 2-dc Cluster in ring, ch 3, (work 3-dc Cluster in ring, ch 3) 5 times; join with slip st to top of first 2-dc Cluster, finish off: 6 ch-3 sps.

Note: Mark Rnd 1 as **right** side.

Rnd 2: With **right** side facing, join Green with slip st in any ch-3 sp; ch 2, work (2-dc Cluster, ch 3, 3-dc Cluster) in same sp, ch 3, (work 3-dc Cluster, ch 3) twice in each ch-3 sp around; join with slip st to top of first 2-dc Cluster, finish off: 12 ch-3 sps.

Rnd 3: With **right** side facing, join Purple with slip st in last ch-3 sp; ch 2, work 2-dc Cluster in same sp, ch 3, (work 3-dc Cluster, ch 3) twice in next ch-3 sp, ★ work 3-dc Cluster in next ch-3 sp, ch 3, (work 3-dc Cluster, ch 3) twice in next ch-3 sp; repeat from ★ around; join with slip st to top of first 2-dc Cluster, finish off: 18 Clusters and 18 ch-3 sps.

Rnd 4: With **right** side facing, join Ecru with slip st in last ch-3 sp; ch 3 **(counts as first dc, now and throughout)**, dc in same sp, 2 dc in next ch-3 sp, (2 dc, ch 2, 2 dc) in next ch-3 sp, ★ 2 dc in each of next 2 ch-3 sps, (2 dc, ch 2, 2 dc) in next ch-3 sp; repeat from ★ around; join with slip st to first dc, finish off: 48 dc and 6 ch-2 sps.

Rnd 5: With **right** side facing, join Green with slip st in any ch-2 sp; ch 4, dc in same sp and in next 8 dc, ★ (dc, ch 1, dc) in next ch-2 sp, dc in next 8 dc; repeat from ★ around; join with slip st to third ch of beginning ch-4: 60 sts and 6 ch-1 sps.

Rnd 6: Ch 3, (2 dc, ch 2, 2 dc) in next ch-1 sp, ★ dc in next 10 dc, (2 dc, ch 2, 2 dc) in next ch-1 sp; repeat from ★ around to last 9 dc, dc in last 9 dc; join with slip st to first dc, finish off: 84 dc and 6 ch-2 sps.

MOTIF C (Make 21)

With Rose, ch 4; join with slip st to form a ring.

Rnd 1 (Right side): Ch 3, work 17 LHDC in ring; join with slip st to top of beginning ch-3, finish off: 18 sts.

Note: Mark Rnd 1 as **right** side.

Rnd 2: With **right** side facing, join Lt Rose with sc in same st as joining *(see Joining With Sc, page 142)*; sc in same st, working in Back Loop *(Fig. 25, page 142)* **and** horizontal strand behind stitch, 2 sc in each LHDC around changing to Green in last sc made *(Fig. 27a, page 142)*; do **not** cut Lt Rose; join with slip st to first sc: 36 sc.

Rnd 3: Ch 4, working over unused strand of Lt Rose, 3 tr in same st, drop Green, ★ with Lt Rose, YO twice, insert hook in same sc, YO and pull up a loop, (YO and draw through 2 loops on hook) twice, † YO twice, insert hook in **next** sc, YO and pull up a loop, (YO and draw through 2 loops on hook) twice †, repeat from † to † 5 times **more**, drop Lt Rose, with Green, YO and draw through all 8 loops on hook **(Petal made)**, working over unused strand of Lt Rose, 7 tr in same sc as last st of Petal, drop Green; repeat from ★ 4 times **more**, with Lt Rose, YO twice, insert hook in same sc, YO and pull up a loop, (YO and draw through 2 loops on hook) twice, repeat from † to † 5 times, YO twice, insert hook in same sc as beginning ch-4, YO and pull up a loop, (YO and draw through 2 loops on hook) twice, cut Lt Rose, with Green, YO and draw through all 8 loops on hook, 3 tr in same st as first tr; join with slip st to top of beginning ch-4, finish off pushing Petals to **right** side: 42 sts and 6 Petals.

Rnd 4: With **right** side facing, join Ecru with slip st in same st as joining; ch 3 **(counts as first dc, now and throughout)**, (dc, ch 2, 2 dc) in same st, dc in next 3 tr, decrease, dc in next 2 tr, ★ (2 dc, ch 2, 2 dc) in next tr, dc in next 3 tr, decrease, dc in next 2 tr; repeat from ★ around; join with slip st to first dc: 60 dc.

Rnd 5: Ch 3, dc in next dc, (2 dc, ch 2, 2 dc) in next ch-2 sp, ★ dc in next 10 dc, (2 dc, ch 2, 2 dc) in next ch-2 sp; repeat from ★ around to last 8 dc, dc in last 8 dc; join with slip st to first dc, finish off: 84 dc and 6 ch-2 sps.

ASSEMBLY

With Ecru, using Placement Diagram as a guide, and working through inside loops only, whipstitch Motifs together *(Fig. 30a, page 143)*, forming 7 vertical strips, beginning in second ch of first corner ch-2 and ending in first ch of next corner ch-2; whipstitch strips together in same manner.

EDGING

With **right** side facing, join Ecru with slip st in any st; work reverse sc in each st around working 2 reverse sc in each ch-2 sp; join with slip st to first st, finish off.

PLACEMENT DIAGRAM

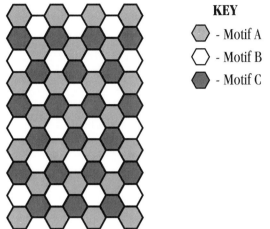

KEY

- Motif A
- Motif B
- Motif C

GARDEN STROLL Continued from page 54.

Rnd 2: With **right** side facing, join Green with sc in same st as joining *(see Joining With Sc, page 142)*; sc in Back Loop Only of next 5 dc *(Fig. 25, page 142)*, working in **front** of next dc, tr around first ch-1 on Row 1 of Center, † ★ skip dc behind tr, sc in Back Loop Only of next 2 dc, working in **front** of next dc, tr around first ch-1 on next row of Center; repeat from ★ across to next corner 6-dc group, sc in Back Loop Only of next 6 dc †, working in **front** of next dc, work FPtr around **both** dc of first Cross St on Row 101 of Center, (skip dc behind FPtr, sc in Back Loop Only of next 2 dc, working in **front** of next dc, work FPtr around **both** dc of next Cross St on Row 101 of Center) 3 times, sc in Back Loop Only of next 6 dc, working in **front** of next dc, tr around first ch-1 on next row of Center, repeat from † to † once, working in **front** of next dc, work FPtr around **both** dc of first Cross St on Row 1 of Center, (skip dc behind FPtr, sc in Back Loop Only of next 2 dc, working in **front** of next dc, work FPtr around **both** dc of next Cross St on Row 1 of Center) 3 times; join with slip st to Back Loop Only of first sc, finish off: 640 sts.

Rnd 3: With **right** side facing and working in Back Loops Only, join Off-White with sc in same st as joining; sc in same st, 2 sc in each of next 3 sc, † sc in next sc, place marker around sc just made for joining placement, sc in same st, 2 sc in next sc, sc in next 298 sts, 2 sc in each of next 2 sc, place marker around last sc made for joining placement, 2 sc in each of next 4 sc, sc in next 10 sts †, 2 sc in each of next 4 sc, repeat from † to † once; join with slip st to **both** loops of first sc, finish off.

ASSEMBLY

Place two Strips with **wrong** sides together and bottom edges at the same end. With Off-White and working through inside loops only, whipstitch Strips together *(Fig. 30a, page 143)*, beginning in first marked sc and ending in next marked sc. Whipstitch remaining Strips together in same manner, always working in same direction.

TRANQUIL GRANNY Continued from page 56.

EDGING

Rnd 1: With **right** side facing, join Black with sc in any corner ch-3 sp *(see Joining With Sc, page 142)*; ch 2, sc in same sp, ★ † ch 1, skip next dc, sc in next dc, ch 1, (sc in next ch-1 sp, ch 1, skip next dc, sc in next dc, ch 1) 3 times, [(sc in next sp, ch 1) twice, skip next dc, sc in next dc, ch 1, (sc in next ch-1 sp, ch 1, skip next dc, sc in next dc, ch 1) 3 times] across to next corner ch-3 sp †, (sc, ch 2, sc) in corner ch-3 sp; repeat from ★ 2 times **more**, then repeat from † to † once; join with slip st to first sc: 396 sps.

Rnd 2: Slip st in first corner ch-2 sp, ch 1, (sc, ch 2, sc) in same sp, ch 1, (sc in next ch-1 sp, ch 1) across to next corner ch-2 sp, ★ (sc, ch 2, sc) in corner ch-2 sp, ch 1, (sc in next ch-1 sp, ch 1) across to next corner ch-2 sp; repeat from ★ 2 times **more**; join with slip st to first sc, finish off: 400 sps.

Rnd 3: With **right** side facing and working across short edge of Afghan, join Blue with slip st in top right corner ch-2 sp; ch 3, 2 dc in same sp, † ch 1, skip next ch-1 sp, (3 dc in next ch-1 sp, ch 1, skip next ch-1 sp) across to next corner ch-2 sp, 3 dc in corner ch-2 sp changing to Lt Blue in last dc *(Fig. 27a, page 142)*, ch 3, 3 dc in same sp, ch 1, skip next ch-1 sp, (3 dc in next ch-1 sp, ch 1, skip next ch-1 sp) across to next corner ch-2 sp †, 3 dc in corner ch-2 sp changing to Blue in last dc, ch 3, 3 dc in same sp, repeat from † to † once, 3 dc in same sp as first dc, ch 3; join with slip st to first dc, finish off.

Rnd 4: With **right** side facing, join Black with slip st in last ch-3 sp made; ch 3, (2 dc, ch 3, 3 dc) in same sp, ch 1, (3 dc in next ch-1 sp, ch 1) across to next corner ch-3 sp, ★ (3 dc, ch 3, 3 dc) in corner ch-3 sp, ch 1, (3 dc in next ch-1 sp, ch 1) across to next corner ch-3 sp; repeat from ★ 2 times **more**; join with slip st to first dc, finish off.

Rnd 5: With **right** side facing, join Green with slip st in first corner ch-3 sp; ch 3, 2 dc in same sp, † ch 1, (3 dc in next ch-1 sp, ch 1) across to next corner ch-3 sp, 3 dc in corner ch-3 sp changing to Lt Green in last dc, ch 3, 3 dc in same sp, ch 1, (3 dc in next ch-1 sp, ch 1) across to next corner ch-3 sp †, 3 dc in corner ch-3 sp changing to Green in last dc, ch 3, 3 dc in same sp, repeat from † to † once, 3 dc in same sp as first dc, ch 3; join with slip st to first dc, finish off.

Rnd 6: With **right** side facing, join Black with slip st in last ch-3 sp made; ch 3, (2 dc, ch 3, 3 dc) in same sp, ch 1, (3 dc in next ch-1 sp, ch 1) across to next corner ch-3 sp, ★ (3 dc, ch 3, 3 dc) in corner ch-3 sp, ch 1, (3 dc in next ch-1 sp, ch 1) across to next corner ch-3 sp; repeat from ★ 2 times **more**; join with slip st to first dc, finish off.

Rnd 7: With **right** side facing, join Purple with slip st in first corner ch-3 sp; ch 3, 2 dc in same sp, † ch 1, (3 dc in next ch-1 sp, ch 1) across to next corner ch-3 sp, 3 dc in corner ch-3 sp changing to Lt Purple in last dc, ch 3, 3 dc in same sp, ch 1, (3 dc in next ch-1 sp, ch 1) across to next corner ch-3 sp †, 3 dc in corner ch-3 sp changing to Purple in last dc, ch 3, 3 dc in same sp, repeat from † to † once, 3 dc in same sp as first dc, ch 3; join with slip st to first dc, finish off.

Rnd 8: With **right** side facing, join Black with slip st in last ch-3 sp made; ch 3, (2 dc, ch 3, 3 dc) in same sp, ch 1, (3 dc in next ch-1 sp, ch 1) across to next corner ch-3 sp, ★ (3 dc, ch 3, 3 dc) in corner ch-3 sp, ch 1, (3 dc in next ch-1 sp, ch 1) across to next corner ch-3 sp; repeat from ★ 2 times **more**; join with slip st to first dc, do **not** finish off.

Rnd 9: Slip st in next dc, ch 1, (slip st, ch 2, slip st) in next corner ch-3 sp, ch 1, ★ skip next dc, slip st in next dc, ch 1, (slip st in next ch-1 sp, ch 1, skip next dc, slip st in next dc, ch 1) across to next corner ch-3 sp, (slip st, ch 2, slip st) in corner ch-3 sp, ch 1; repeat from ★ 2 times **more**, skip next dc, (slip st in next dc, ch 1, slip st in next ch-1 sp, ch 1, skip next st) across; join with slip st to first slip st, finish off.

Rnd 9: With **right** side facing, join Ecru with sc in first sc to left of any Cluster; ★ † (working in **front** of next ch-3, dc in next 3 sts one rnd **below** ch-3, sc in next sc) 4 times, working **behind** next Cluster, (dc, ch 3, dc) in sp **before** next sc one rnd **below** Cluster †, sc in next sc; repeat from ★ 2 times **more**, then repeat from † to † once; join with slip st to first sc, finish off: 76 sts and 4 ch-3 sps.

ASSEMBLY

With Ecru and working through both loops, whipstitch Squares together *(Fig. 30b, page 143)*, forming 7 vertical strips of 9 Squares each, beginning in center ch of first corner ch-3 and ending in center ch of next corner ch-3; whipstitch strips together in same manner.

EDGING

Rnd 1: With **right** side facing, join Ecru with slip st in any corner ch-3 sp; ch 3 **(counts as first dc)**, (dc, ch 3, 2 dc) in same sp, dc in next 19 sts, (dc in next sp and in next joining, dc in next sp and in next 19 sts) across to next corner ch-3 sp, ★ (2 dc, ch 3, 2 dc) in corner ch-3 sp, dc in next 19 sts, (dc in next sp and in next joining, dc in next sp and in next 19 sts) across to next corner ch-3 sp; repeat from ★ 2 times **more**; join with slip st to first dc, finish off: 708 dc and 4 ch-3 sps.

Rnd 2: With **wrong** side facing, join Rose with sc in any corner ch-3 sp; work Corner Cluster, sc in same sp, work Cluster, skip next 3 dc, (sc in next dc, work Cluster, skip next 3 dc) across to next corner ch-3 sp, ★ (sc, work Corner Cluster, sc) in corner ch-3 sp, work Cluster, skip next 3 dc, (sc in next dc, work Cluster, skip next 3 dc) across to next corner ch-3 sp; repeat from ★ 2 times **more**; join with slip st to first sc, finish off: 178 Clusters and 4 Corner Clusters.

Rnd 3: With **right** side facing, join Ecru with sc in first sc to left of any Corner Cluster; ★ † (working **behind** next Cluster, dc in next 3 dc one rnd **below** Cluster, sc in next sc) across to next Corner Cluster, working **behind** Corner Cluster, (dc, ch 3, dc) in sp **before** next sc one rnd **below** Corner Cluster †, sc in next sc; repeat from ★ 2 times **more**, then repeat from † to † once; join with slip st to first sc, finish off: 724 sts and 4 ch-3 sps.

Rnd 4: With **wrong** side facing, join Green with sc in any corner ch-3 sp; work Corner Cluster, sc in same sp, work Cluster, skip next 3 sts, (sc in next dc, work Cluster, skip next 3 sts) across to next corner ch-3 sp, ★ (sc, work Corner Cluster, sc) in corner ch-3 sp, work Cluster, skip next 3 sts, (sc in next dc, work Cluster, skip next 3 sts) across to next corner ch-3 sp; repeat from ★ 2 times **more**; join with slip st to first sc, finish off: 182 Clusters and 4 Corner Clusters.

Rnd 5: Repeat Rnd 3: 740 sts and 4 ch-3 sps.

Rnd 6: Repeat Rnd 2: 186 Clusters and 4 Corner Clusters.

Rnd 7: Repeat Rnd 3; do **not** finish off: 756 sts and 4 ch-3 sps.

Rnd 8: Ch 1, sc in same st, ★ ch 1, skip next dc, (sc in next st, ch 1, skip next dc) across to next corner ch-3 sp, (sc, ch 2, sc) in corner ch-3 sp; repeat from ★ around; join with slip st to first sc: 384 sc and 384 sps.

Rnd 9: Slip st in first ch-1 sp, ch 1, ★ (slip st in next ch-1 sp, ch 1) across to next corner ch-2 sp, (slip st, ch 2, slip st) in corner ch-2 sp, ch 1; repeat from ★ around; join with slip st to first slip st, finish off.

SUMMER SYMPHONY

Rosy stripes provide a soft accent for this rippled throw, which looks crisp and inviting crocheted in white and shades of green. What a beautiful symphony of summer color!

Finished Size: 49" x 66"

MATERIALS

Worsted Weight Yarn:
- Dk Green - 13 ounces, (370 grams, 855 yards)
- White - 13 ounces, (370 grams, 855 yards)
- Green - 10 ounces, (280 grams, 655 yards)
- Pink - 5 ounces, (140 grams, 330 yards)

Crochet hook, size H (5.00 mm) **or** size needed for gauge

GAUGE: Each repeat from point to point = 3¼"; 7 rows = 5"

Gauge Swatch: 7"w x 5"h
Ch 35 **loosely**.
Work same as Afghan for 7 rows.
Finish off.

STITCH GUIDE

CLUSTER (uses next 5 sts)
YO, insert hook in next st, YO and pull up a loop, YO and draw through 2 loops on hook, YO, skip next 3 sts or ch-1 sps, insert hook in next st, YO and pull up a loop, YO and draw through 2 loops on hook, YO and draw through all 3 loops on hook *(Fig. 15b, page 140)*.

DECREASE (uses next 3 sts)
YO, insert hook in next dc, YO and pull up a loop, YO and draw through 2 loops on hook, YO, skip next st, insert hook in next dc, YO and pull up a loop, YO and draw through 2 loops on hook, YO and draw through all 3 loops on hook.

COLOR SEQUENCE

One row Dk Green *(Fig. 27a, page 142)*, 3 rows White, one row Dk Green, ★ one row Green, one row Pink, one row Green, one row Dk Green, 3 rows White, one row Dk Green; repeat from ★ throughout.

With Dk Green, ch 230 **loosely**.

Row 1 (Right side): Dc in fifth ch from hook **(4 skipped chs count as first dc plus one skipped ch)** and in next 5 chs, 2 dc in next ch, ch 3, 2 dc in next ch, ★ dc in next 4 chs, work Cluster, dc in next 4 chs, 2 dc in next ch, ch 3, 2 dc in next ch; repeat from ★ across to last 8 chs, dc in next 6 chs, skip next ch, dc in last ch: 200 sts and 15 ch-3 sps.

Note: Loop a short piece of yarn around any stitch to mark Row 1 as **right** side.

Row 2: Ch 3 **(counts as first dc, now and throughout)**, turn; working in both loops, skip next 2 dc, dc in next dc, ch 1, skip next dc, (dc in next dc, ch 1, skip next dc) twice, (dc, ch 3, dc) in next ch-3 sp, ★ ch 1, skip next dc, (dc in next dc, ch 1, skip next dc) twice, decrease, ch 1, skip next dc, (dc in next dc, ch 1, skip next dc) twice, (dc, ch 3, dc) in next ch-3 sp; repeat from ★ across to last 9 dc, (ch 1, skip next dc, dc in next dc) 3 times, skip next 2 dc, dc in last dc: 108 sts and 105 sps.

Row 3: Ch 3, turn; skip next dc, (dc in next ch-1 sp and in next dc) 3 times, (2 dc, ch 3, 2 dc) in next ch-3 sp, ★ (dc in next dc and in next ch-1 sp) twice, work Cluster, (dc in next ch-1 sp and in next dc) twice, (2 dc, ch 3, 2 dc) in next ch-3 sp; repeat from ★ across to last 8 sts, (dc in next dc and in next ch-1 sp) 3 times, skip next dc, dc in last dc: 200 sts and 15 ch-3 sps.

Rows 4 and 5: Repeat Rows 2 and 3.

Rows 6-9: Ch 3, turn; working in Back Loops Only *(Fig. 25, page 142)*, skip next 2 dc, dc in next 6 dc, (2 dc, ch 3, 2 dc) in next ch-3 sp, ★ dc in next 4 dc, work Cluster, dc in next 4 dc, (2 dc, ch 3, 2 dc) in next ch-3 sp; repeat from ★ across to last 9 dc, dc in next 6 dc, skip next 2 dc, dc in last dc.

Rows 10-93: Repeat Rows 2-9, 10 times, then repeat Rows 2-5 once **more**.
Finish off.

Holding 9 strands of Dk Green together, add fringe at each point across short edges of Afghan *(Figs. 31a & c, page 143)*.

RESTFUL WRAP

Evocative of summer leaves and lawns, the green and off-white blocks in this wrap create a restful pattern. Front post and back post double crochets give the afghan an interesting texture.

Finished Size: 47" x 67"

MATERIALS
Worsted Weight Yarn:
Off-White - 51 ounces, (1,450 grams, 2,975 yards)
Green - 26 ounces, (740 grams, 1,515 yards)
Crochet hook, size H (5.00 mm) **or** size needed
for gauge
Yarn needle

GAUGE: Each Square = 5"

Gauge Swatch: 3¹/₂"
Work same as Square A through Rnd 3.

STITCH GUIDE

BACK POST DOUBLE CROCHET *(abbreviated BPdc)*
YO, insert hook from **back** to **front** around post of st indicated, YO and pull up a loop *(Fig. 14, page 139)*, (YO and draw through 2 loops on hook) twice. Skip st in front of BPdc.

FRONT POST DOUBLE CROCHET
(abbreviated FPdc)
YO, insert hook from **front** to **back** around post of st indicated, YO and pull up a loop *(Fig. 11, page 139)*, (YO and draw through 2 loops on hook) twice. Skip st behind FPdc.

SQUARE A (Make 59)

With Off-White, ch 4; join with slip st to form a ring.
Rnd 1 (Right side)**:** Ch 3 **(counts as first dc, now and throughout)**, 2 dc in ring, ch 2, (3 dc in ring, ch 2) 3 times; join with slip st to first dc: 12 dc.
Note: Loop a short piece of yarn around any stitch to mark Rnd 1 as **right** side.
Rnd 2: Ch 3, dc in next 2 dc, (2 dc, ch 2, 2 dc) in next ch-2 sp, ★ dc in next 3 dc, (2 dc, ch 2, 2 dc) in next ch-2 sp; repeat from ★ around; join with slip st to first dc: 28 dc.

Rnd 3: Ch 3, dc in next 4 dc, (2 dc, ch 2, 2 dc) in next ch-2 sp, ★ dc in next 7 dc, (2 dc, ch 2, 2 dc) in next ch-2 sp; repeat from ★ around to last 2 dc, dc in last 2 dc; join with slip st to first dc, finish off: 44 dc.
Rnd 4: With **right** side facing, join Green with slip st in any ch-2 sp; ch 3, (dc, ch 2, 2 dc) in same sp, work BPdc around next dc, (work FPdc around next dc, work BPdc around next dc) across to next ch-2 sp, ★ (2 dc, ch 2, 2 dc) in ch-2 sp, work BPdc around next dc, (work FPdc around next dc, work BPdc around next dc) across to next ch-2 sp; repeat from ★ around; join with slip st to first dc, finish off: 60 sts and 4 ch-2 sps.
Rnd 5: With **right** side facing, join Off-White with sc in first st *(see Joining With Sc, page 142)*; sc in next dc and in each st around working 3 sc in each ch-2 sp; join with slip st to first sc, finish off: 72 sc.

SQUARE B (Make 58)

With Green, ch 4; join with slip st to form a ring.
Rnd 1 (Right side)**:** Ch 3, 2 dc in ring, ch 2, (3 dc in ring, ch 2) 3 times; join with slip st to first dc: 12 dc.
Note: Mark Rnd 1 as **right** side.
Rnd 2: Ch 1, sc in same st and in next 2 dc, slip st in next 2 chs, (sc in next 3 dc, slip st in next 2 chs) around; join with slip st to first sc, finish off: 20 sts.
Rnd 3: With **right** side facing, working over slip sts and into ch-2 sps on Rnd 1 and around dc on Rnd 1, join Off-White with slip st in any ch-2 sp; ch 3, (dc, ch 2, 2 dc) in same sp, work FPdc around next dc, work BPdc around next dc, work FPdc around next dc, ★ (2 dc, ch 2, 2 dc) in next ch-2 sp, work FPdc around next dc, work BPdc around next dc, work FPdc around next dc; repeat from ★ around; join with slip st to first dc: 28 sts and 4 ch-2 sps.
Rnd 4: Ch 1, sc in same st and in next dc, slip st in next 2 chs, (sc in next 7 sts, slip st in next 2 chs) 3 times, sc in last 5 sts; join with slip st to first sc, finish off: 36 sts.

Continued on page 76.

ABSOLUTELY GORGEOUS

Absolutely gorgeous in sky blue, this fanciful throw features a lacy pattern of fans. A wide scalloped edging enhances its Victorian elegance.

Finished Size: 48" x 63"

MATERIALS
Worsted Weight Yarn:
  51 ounces, (1,450 grams, 2,465 yards)
Crochet hook, size G (4.00 mm) **or** size needed
  for gauge

GAUGE: In pattern, one repeat = 2³/₄";
        4 rows = 2"

Gauge Swatch: 6¹/₄"w x 4"h
Ch 31 **loosely**.
Work same as Afghan for 8 rows.
Finish off.

AFGHAN BODY

Ch 163 **loosely**.
Row 1: Dc in seventh ch from hook **(6 skipped chs count as first dc plus ch 3)**, place marker in same ch for st placement, ch 3, skip next 3 chs, sc in next 5 chs, ch 3, ★ skip next 3 chs, (dc, ch 3) twice in next ch, skip next 3 chs, sc in next 5 chs, ch 3; repeat from ★ across to last 4 chs, skip next 3 chs, (dc, ch 3, dc) in last ch: 93 sts and 40 ch-3 sps.
Row 2 (Right side)**:** Ch 4 **(counts as first tr)**, turn; 4 tr in first ch-3 sp, ch 1, skip next sc, sc in next 3 sc, ch 1, ★ skip next ch-3 sp, 9 tr in next ch-3 sp, ch 1, skip next sc, sc in next 3 sc, ch 1; repeat from ★ across to last 2 ch-3 sps, skip next ch-3 sp, 4 tr in last ch-3 sp, tr in last dc: 118 tr and 39 sc.
Row 3: Ch 1, turn; sc in first 3 tr, ch 3, (dc, ch 3) twice in center sc of next 3-sc group, ★ skip next sc and next 2 tr, sc in next 5 tr, ch 3, (dc, ch 3) twice in center sc of next 3-sc group; repeat from ★ across to last sc, skip next sc and next 2 tr, sc in last 3 tr: 92 sts and 39 ch-3 sps.

Row 4: Ch 1, turn; sc in first 2 sc, ch 1, skip next ch-3 sp, 9 tr in next ch-3 sp, ch 1, ★ skip next sc, sc in next 3 sc, ch 1, skip next ch-3 sp, 9 tr in next ch-3 sp, ch 1; repeat from ★ across to last 3 sc, skip next sc, sc in last 2 sc: 117 tr and 40 sc.
Row 5: Ch 6 **(counts as first dc plus ch 3)**, turn; dc in same st, ch 3, skip next sc and next 2 tr, sc in next 5 tr, ch 3, ★ (dc, ch 3) twice in center sc of next 3-sc group, skip next sc and next 2 tr, sc in next 5 tr, ch 3; repeat from ★ across to last 2 sc, skip next sc, (dc, ch 3, dc) in last sc: 93 sts and 40 ch-3 sps.
Rows 6-103: Repeat Rows 2-5, 24 times; then repeat Rows 2 and 3 once **more**; do **not** finish off.

EDGING

Rnd 1: Ch 1, turn; 2 sc in first sc, ch 3, 3 sc in next ch-3 sp, ch 3, ★ skip next ch-3 sp, (3 sc in next ch-3 sp, ch 3) twice; repeat from ★ across to last 2 ch-3 sps, skip next ch-3 sp, 3 sc in last ch-3 sp, ch 3, skip next 2 sc, 3 sc in last sc, ch 3; working in end of rows, skip first 2 rows, 3 sc in next row, ch 3, skip next 2 rows, 3 sc in next row, ch 3, † skip next row, sc in next row, 2 sc in next row, ch 3, skip next row, 3 sc in next row, ch 3, skip next 2 rows, 3 sc in next row, ch 3 †, repeat from † to † across to last row, skip last row; working in free loops of beginning ch **(Fig. 26b, page 142)**, 3 sc in marked ch, ch 3, skip next ch, sc in next 3 chs, ch 3, (skip next 3 chs, sc in next 3 chs, ch 3) across to last 2 chs, skip next ch, 3 sc in last ch, ch 3; working in end of rows, skip first row, 3 sc in next row, ch 3, skip next 2 rows, 3 sc in next row, ch 3, repeat from † to † across to last 2 rows, skip last 2 rows, sc in same st as first sc; join with slip st to first sc, do **not** finish off: 396 sc and 132 ch-3 sps.

Continued on page 77.

CIRCLE OF ROSES

*Lush pink roses adorn this beautiful throw fashioned in honor of
National Rose Month (June). The floral motifs are joined as you crochet.*

Finished Size: 51" x 68"

MATERIALS
Worsted Weight Yarn:
> Ecru - 23 ounces, (650 grams, 1,575 yards)
> Peach - 11½ ounces, (330 grams, 790 yards)
> Green - 10 ounces, (280 grams, 685 yards)

Crochet hook, size G (4.00 mm) **or** size needed
for gauge

GAUGE: Each Motif = 8" in diameter

Gauge Swatch: 2½"
Work same as First Motif Center through Rnd 3.

STITCH GUIDE

> **PICOT**
> Ch 1, sc in top of st just made.

MOTIF (Make 52)
With Peach, ch 6; join with slip st to form a ring.
Rnd 1 (Right side): Ch 1, 12 sc in ring; join with slip st to first
sc: 12 sc.
Note: Loop a short piece of yarn around any stitch to mark
Rnd 1 as **right** side.
Rnd 2: Ch 1, sc in same st, ch 3, skip next sc, ★ sc in next sc,
ch 3, skip next sc; repeat from ★ around; join with slip st to
first sc: 6 ch-3 sps.
Rnd 3: Slip st in first ch-3 sp, ch 1, [sc, ch 1, (dc, ch 1) 3
times, sc] in same sp and in each ch-3 sp around; join with
slip st to first sc: 6 petals.
Rnd 4: Ch 1, keeping petals in **front** of work, sc around post of
sc on Rnd 2 **below** same st as joining *(Fig. 9, page 139)*,
ch 4, (sc around post of next sc on Rnd 2, ch 4) around; join
with slip st to first sc: 6 ch-4 sps.
Rnd 5: Slip st in first ch-4 sp, ch 1, [sc, ch 1, (dc, ch 1) 5
times, sc] in same sp and in each ch-4 sp around; join with
slip st to first sc: 6 petals.

Rnd 6: Ch 1, keeping petals in **front** of work, sc around post of
sc on Rnd 4 **below** same st as joining, ch 7, (sc around post of
next sc on Rnd 4, ch 7) around; join with slip st to first sc,
finish off: 6 ch-7 sps.
Rnd 7: With **right** side facing, join Green with sc in any ch-7 sp
(see Joining With Sc, page 142); ch 5, sc in same sp, (ch 5,
sc) twice in each ch-7 sp around, ch 2, dc in first sc to form last
ch-5 sp: 12 ch-5 sps.
Rnd 8: Ch 1, sc in same sp, (ch 5, sc in next ch-5 sp) around,
ch 1, tr in first sc to form last ch-5 sp.
Rnd 9: Ch 1, (sc, work Picot, sc) in same sp, ch 11, ★ (sc,
work Picot, sc) in next ch-5 sp, ch 11; repeat from ★ around;
join with slip st to first sc, finish off.

FIRST CIRCLE
RING
With Ecru, ch 8 **loosely**.
Row 1: Dc in sixth ch from hook and in last 2 chs: 3 dc and
one ch-5 sp.
Row 2 (Right side - Joining row): Ch 2, turn; with **wrong** side
of any Motif facing, sc in fourth ch of any ch-11 *(Fig. 29,
page 142)*, ch 2, dc in first dc and in each dc across Ring.
Row 3: Ch 5, turn; dc in first dc and in each dc across.
Row 4 (Joining row): Ch 2, turn; with **wrong** side of Motif
facing, skip next 3 chs from last joining, sc in next ch, ch 2, dc
in first dc and in each dc across Ring.
Row 5: Ch 5, turn; dc in first dc and in each dc across.
Row 6: Ch 2, turn; with **wrong** side of Motif facing, sc in fourth
ch of next ch-11, ch 2, dc in first dc and in each dc across Ring.
Rows 7-48: Repeat Rows 3-6, 10 times; then repeat
Rows 3 and 4 once **more**.
Joining: Ch 1, turn; with **right** side of Ring together, working in
free loops of beginning ch at base of dc on Row 1 *(Fig. 26b,
page 142)* **and** through both loops of dc on Row 48, slip st
loosely in each st across; finish off.

Continued on page 74.

SECOND CIRCLE

RING

With Ecru, ch 8 **loosely**.

Row 1: Dc in sixth ch from hook and in last 2 chs: 3 dc and one ch-5 sp.

Row 2 (Right side - Joining row)**:** Ch 2, turn; with **wrong** side of any Motif facing, sc in fourth ch of any ch-11, ch 2, dc in first dc and in each dc across Ring.

Row 3: Ch 5, turn; dc in first dc and in each dc across.

Row 4 (Joining row)**:** Ch 2, turn; with **wrong** side of Motif facing, skip next 3 chs from last joining, sc in next ch, ch 2, dc in first dc and in each dc across Ring.

Row 5: Ch 5, turn; dc in first dc and in each dc across.

Row 6: Ch 2, turn; with **wrong** side of Motif facing, sc in fourth ch of next ch-11, ch 2, dc in first dc and in each dc across Ring.

Rows 7-40: Repeat Rows 3-6, 8 times; then repeat Rows 3 and 4 once **more**.

Row 41: Ch 2, do **not** turn; holding **previous Circle** with **wrong** side facing, sc in any corresponding ch-5 sp on Ring, ch 2, turn; dc in first dc and in each dc across ring on **new Circle**.

Row 42: Ch 2, turn; with **wrong** side of **Motif** facing, sc in fourth ch of next ch-11, ch 2, dc in first dc and in each dc across **Ring**.

Row 43: Ch 2, do **not** turn; holding **previous Circle** with **wrong** side facing, sc in next corresponding ch-5 sp on Ring, ch 2, turn; dc in first dc and in each dc across on Ring of **new Circle**.

Row 44: Ch 2, turn; with **wrong** side of **Motif** facing, skip next 3 chs from last joining, sc in next ch, ch 2, dc in first dc and in each dc across **Ring**.

Row 45: Repeat Row 43.

Row 46: Repeat Row 42.

Rows 47 and 48: Repeat Rows 43 and 44.

Joining: Ch 1, turn; with **right** side of Ring together, working in free loops of beginning ch at base of dc on Row 1 **and** through both loops of dc on Row 48, slip st **loosely** in each st across; finish off.

ADDITIONAL CIRCLES

RING

Note: Following Placement Diagram, page 75, work One, Two, or Three Side Joining. To complete the first Strip, work and join 5 **more** Circles, skipping 8 ch-5 sps on previous Circle when joining. Work and join remaining Circles in same manner, skipping ch-5 sps as indicated on Placement Diagram.

ONE SIDE JOINING

Rows 1-6: Work same as Second Circle.

Rows 7-40: Repeat Rows 3-6, 8 times; then repeat Rows 3 and 4 once **more**.

Row 41: Ch 2, do **not** turn; holding **previous Circle** with **wrong** side facing, sc in corresponding ch-5 sp on Ring, ch 2, turn; dc in first dc and in each dc across Ring on **new Circle**.

Row 42: Ch 2, turn; with **wrong** side of **Motif** facing, sc in fourth ch of next ch-11, ch 2, dc in first dc and in each dc across **Ring**.

Row 43: Ch 2, do **not** turn; holding **previous Circle** with **wrong** side facing, sc in next corresponding ch-5 sp on Ring, ch 2, turn; dc in first dc and in each dc across Ring of **new Circle**.

Row 44: Ch 2, turn; with **wrong** side of **Motif** facing, skip next 3 chs from last joining, sc in next ch, ch 2, dc in first dc and in each dc across **Ring**.

Row 45: Repeat Row 43.

Row 46: Repeat Row 42.

Rows 47 and 48: Repeat Rows 43 and 44.

Joining: Ch 1, turn; with **right** side of Ring together, working in free loops of beginning ch at base of dc on Row 1 **and** through both loops of dc on Row 48, slip st **loosely** in each st across; finish off.

TWO SIDE JOINING

Rows 1-6: Work same as Second Circle.

Rows 7-32: Repeat Rows 3-6, 6 times; then repeat Rows 3 and 4 once **more**.

Row 33: Ch 2, do **not** turn; holding **previous Circle** with **wrong** side facing, sc in corresponding ch-5 sp on Ring, ch 2, turn; dc in first dc and in each dc across Ring on **new Circle**.

Row 34: Ch 2, turn; with **wrong** side of **Motif** facing, sc in fourth ch of next ch-11, ch 2, dc in first dc and in each dc across **Ring**.

Row 35: Ch 2, do **not** turn; holding **previous Circle** with **wrong** side facing, sc in next corresponding ch-5 sp on Ring, ch 2, turn; dc in first dc and in each dc across Ring of **new Circle**.

Row 36: Ch 2, turn; with **wrong** side of **Motif** facing, skip next 3 chs from last joining, sc in next ch, ch 2, dc in first dc and in each dc across **Ring**.

Row 37: Repeat Row 35.

Row 38: Repeat Row 34.

Rows 39 and 40: Repeat Rows 35 and 36.

Row 41: Ch 2, do **not** turn; holding next **previous Circle** with **wrong** side facing, sc in next corresponding ch-5 sp on Ring, ch 2, turn; dc in first dc and in each dc across ring of **new Circle**.

Rows 42-48: Repeat Rows 34-40.

Joining: Ch 1, turn; with **right** side of Ring together, working in free loops of beginning ch at base of dc on Row 1 **and** through both loops of dc on Row 48, slip st **loosely** in each st across; finish off.

THREE SIDE JOINING

Rows 1-6: Work same as Second Circle.

Rows 7-24: Repeat Rows 3-6, 4 times, then repeat Rows 3 and 4 once **more**.

Row 25: Ch 2, do **not** turn; holding **previous Circle** with **wrong** side facing, sc in corresponding ch-5 sp on Ring, ch 2, turn; dc in first dc and in each dc across Ring on **new Circle**.

Row 26: Ch 2, turn; with **wrong** side of **Motif** facing, sc in fourth ch of next ch-11, ch 2, dc in first dc and in each dc across **Ring**.

Row 27: Ch 2, do **not** turn; holding **previous Circle** with **wrong** side facing, sc in next corresponding ch-5 sp on Ring, ch 2, turn; dc in first dc and in each dc across Ring of **new Circle**.

Row 28: Ch 2, turn; with **wrong** side of **Motif** facing, skip next 3 chs from last joining, sc in next ch, ch 2, dc in first dc and in each dc across **Ring**.

Row 29: Repeat Row 27.

Row 30: Repeat Row 26.

Rows 31 and 32: Repeat Rows 27 and 28.

Row 33: Ch 2, do **not** turn; holding next **previous Circle** with **wrong** side facing, sc in next corresponding ch-5 sp on Ring, ch 2, turn; dc in first dc and in each dc across ring of **new Circle**.

Row 33: Ch 2, do **not** turn; holding next **previous Circle** with **wrong** side facing, sc in next corresponding ch-5 sp on Ring, ch 2, turn; dc in first dc and in each dc across ring of **new Circle**.

Rows 34-48: Repeat Rows 26-33 once, then repeat Rows 26-32 once **more**.

Joining: Ch 1, turn; with **right** side of Ring together, working in free loops of beginning ch at base of dc on Row 1 **and** through both loops of dc on Row 48, slip st **loosely** in each st across; finish off.

EDGING

Rnd 1: With **right** side facing, join Ecru with sc in ch-5 sp to left of any joining; (ch 5, sc in next ch-5 sp) across to next joining, ch 3, skip joining, ★ sc in next ch-5 sp, (ch 5, sc in next ch-5 sp) across to next joining, ch 3, skip joining; repeat from ★ around; join with slip st to first sc, finish off: 216 sps.

Rnd 2: With **right** side facing, join Green with sc in first ch-5 sp; work Picot, sc in same sp, [ch 5, (sc, work Picot, sc) in next ch-5 sp] across to next ch-3 sp, skip ch-3 sp, ★ (sc, work Picot, sc) in next ch-5 sp, [ch 5, (sc, work Picot, sc) in next ch-5 sp] across to next ch-3 sp, skip ch-3 sp; repeat from ★ around; join with slip st to first sc, finish off: 168 ch-5 sps.

Rnd 3: With **right** side facing, join Ecru with sc in first ch-5 sp; 2 sc in same sp, ch 5, (3 sc in next ch-5 sp, ch 5) around; join with slip st to first sc: 504 sc.

Rnd 4: Slip st in next sc, ch 1, sc in same st, (dc, ch 2, tr, work Picot, tr, ch 2, dc) in next ch-5 sp, skip next sc, ★ sc in next sc, (dc, ch 2, tr, work Picot, tr, ch 2, dc) in next ch-5 sp, skip next sc; repeat from ★ around; join with slip st to first sc, finish off.

PLACEMENT DIAGRAM

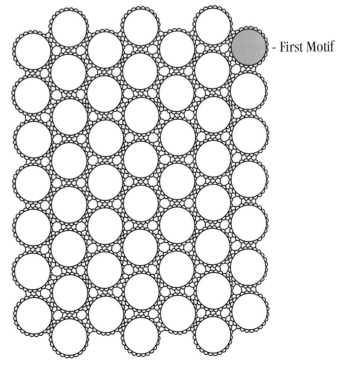

- First Motif

75

Rnd 5: With **right** side facing, working over slip sts and into ch-2 sps on Rnd 3 and around sts on Rnd 3, join Green with slip st in any ch-2 sp; ch 3, (dc, ch 2, 2 dc) in same sp, work FPdc around next dc, (work BPdc around next st, work FPdc around next st) 3 times, ★ (2 dc, ch 2, 2 dc) in next ch-2 sp, work FPdc around next dc, (work BPdc around next st, work FPdc around next st) 3 times; repeat from ★ around; join with slip st to first dc: 44 sts and 4 ch-2 sps.

Rnd 6: Ch 1, sc in same st and in next dc, slip st in next 2 chs, (sc in next 11 sts, slip st in next 2 chs) 3 times, sc in last 9 sts; join with slip st to first sc, finish off: 52 sts.

Rnd 7: With **right** side facing, working over slip sts and into ch-2 sps on Rnd 5 and around sts on Rnd 5, join Off-White with slip st in any ch-2 sp; ch 3, (dc, ch 2, 2 dc) in same sp, work FPdc around next dc, (work BPdc around next st, work FPdc around next st) across to next ch-2 sp, ★ (2 dc, ch 2, 2 dc) in ch-2 sp, work FPdc around next dc, (work BPdc around next st, work FPdc around next st) across to next ch-2 sp; repeat from ★ around; join with slip st to first dc: 60 sts and 4 ch-2 sps.

Rnd 8: Ch 1, sc in same st and in each st around working 3 sc in each ch-2 sp; join with slip st to first sc, finish off: 72 sc.

ASSEMBLY

With Off-White, using Placement Diagram as a guide, and working through inside loops only, whipstitch Squares together *(Fig. 30a, page 143)*, forming 9 vertical strips of 13 Squares each, beginning in center sc of first corner and ending in center sc of next corner; whipstitch strips together in same manner.

EDGING

Rnd 1: With **right** side facing and working in Back Loops Only *(Fig. 25, page 142)*, join Off-White with sc in center sc of any corner 3-sc group; 2 sc in same st, ★ † sc in next 17 sts, (sc in same st as joining on same Square and in same st as joining on next Square, sc in next 17 sts) across to center sc of next corner 3-sc group †, 3 sc in center sc; repeat from ★ 2 times **more**, then repeat from † to † once; join with slip st to **both** loops of first sc, finish off.

Rnd 2: With **right** side facing and working in both loops, join Green with sc in any sc; sc in next sc and in each sc around working 3 sc in center sc of each corner 3-sc group; join with slip st to first sc, finish off.

Rnd 3: With **right** side facing and working in Back Loops Only, join Off-White with sc in any sc; sc in next sc and in each sc around working 3 sc in center sc of each corner 3-sc group; join with slip st to **both** loops of first sc, finish off.

PLACEMENT DIAGRAM

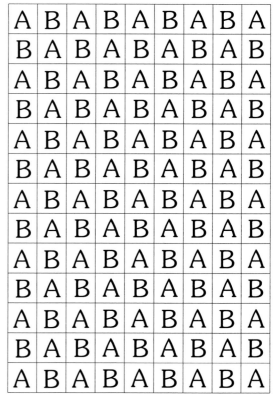

Rnd 2: Ch 1, do **not** turn; sc in same st, 5 dc in next ch-3 sp, (sc in center sc of next 3-sc group, 5 dc in next ch-3 sp) around; join with slip st to first sc: 132 sc and 660 dc.

Rnd 3: Slip st in next 2 dc, ch 1, sc in same st and in next 2 dc, ★ † (ch 3, skip next 3 sts, sc in next 3 dc) across to within one dc of next corner sc, ch 5, skip next 3 sts †, sc in next 3 dc; repeat from ★ 2 times **more**, then repeat from † to † once; join with slip st to first sc: 396 sc and 132 sps.

Rnd 4: Slip st in next sc, ch 1, sc in same st, 5 dc in next ch-3 sp, ★ sc in center sc of next 3-sc group, (5 dc in next ch-3 sp, sc in center sc of next 3-sc group) across to next corner ch-5 sp, 9 dc in corner ch-5 sp; repeat from ★ around; join with slip st to first sc: 132 sc and 676 dc.

Rnd 5: Ch 5 **(counts as first dc plus ch 2, now and throughout)**, dc in same st, ch 2, † skip next 2 dc, sc in next dc, ch 2, [skip next 2 dc, (dc, ch 2) twice in next sc, skip next 2 dc, sc in next dc, ch 2] 26 times, skip next dc, (dc, ch 3, dc) in next dc, ch 2, skip next dc, sc in next dc, ch 2, [skip next 2 dc, (dc, ch 2) twice in next sc, skip next 2 dc, sc in next dc, ch 2] 39 times, skip next dc, (dc, ch 3, dc) in next dc, ch 2, skip next dc, sc in next dc, ch 2, skip next 2 dc †, (dc, ch 2) twice in next sc, repeat from † to † once; join with slip st to first dc: 408 sts and 408 sps.

Rnd 6: Slip st in first ch-2 sp, ch 5, dc in same sp, ch 2, ★ † skip next 2 ch-2 sps, [8 tr in next ch-2 sp, ch 2, skip next 2 ch-2 sps, (dc, ch 2) twice in next ch-2 sp, skip next 2 ch-2 sps] across to next corner ch-3 sp, 16 tr in corner ch-3 sp, ch 2, skip next 2 ch-2 sps †, (dc, ch 2) twice in next ch-2 sp; repeat from ★ 2 times **more**, then repeat from † to † once; join with slip st to first dc: 712 sts and 204 sps.

Rnd 7: Slip st in first ch-2 sp, ch 5, dc in same sp, ch 2, † skip next dc and next 2 tr, [tr in sp **before** next tr *(Fig. 28, page 142)*, skip next tr] twice, 4 tr in sp **before** next tr, (skip next tr, tr in sp **before** next tr) twice, [ch 2, skip next ch-2 sp, (dc, ch 2) twice in next ch-2 sp, skip next dc and next 2 tr, (tr in sp **before** next tr, skip next tr) twice, 4 tr in sp **before** next tr, (skip next tr, tr in sp **before** next tr) twice] 13 times, ch 1, skip next 2 tr, (dc, ch 2, dc) in sp **before** next tr, ch 1, skip next 2 tr, (tr in sp **before** next tr, skip next tr) twice, 4 tr in sp **before** next tr, (skip next tr, tr in sp **before** next tr) twice, [ch 2, skip next ch-2 sp, (dc, ch 2) twice in next ch-2 sp, skip next dc and next 2 tr, (tr in sp **before** next tr, skip next tr) twice, 4 tr in sp **before** next tr, (skip next tr, tr in sp **before** next tr) twice] 20 times, ch 1, skip next 2 tr, (dc, ch 2, dc) in sp **before** next tr, ch 1, skip next 2 tr, (tr in sp **before** next tr, skip next tr) twice, 4 tr in sp **before** next tr, (skip next tr, tr in sp **before** next tr) twice, ch 2, skip next ch-2 sp †, (dc, ch 2) twice in next ch-2 sp, repeat from † to † once; join with slip st to first dc: 720 sts and 216 sps.

Rnds 8-10: Slip st in first ch-2 sp, ch 5, dc in same sp, ch 2, skip next dc and next 2 tr, (tr in sp **before** next tr, skip next tr) twice, 4 tr in sp **before** next tr, (skip next tr, tr in sp **before** next tr) twice, ch 2, ★ skip next sp, (dc, ch 2) twice in next ch-2 sp, skip next dc and next 2 tr, (tr in sp **before** next tr, skip next tr) twice, 4 tr in sp **before** next tr, (skip next tr, tr in sp **before** next tr) twice, ch 2; repeat from ★ around; join with slip st to first dc.

Rnd 11: Slip st in first ch-2 sp, ch 1, sc in same sp, ch 4, skip next dc and next tr, sc in sp **before** next tr, ch 4, skip next 3 tr, (sc, ch 5, sc) in sp **before** next tr, ch 4, skip next 3 tr, sc in sp **before** next tr, ch 4, skip next ch-2 sp, ★ sc in next ch-2 sp, ch 4, skip next dc and next tr, sc in sp **before** next tr, ch 4, skip next 3 tr, (sc, ch 5, sc) in sp **before** next tr, ch 4, skip next 3 tr, sc in sp **before** next tr, ch 4, skip next ch-2 sp; repeat from ★ around; join with slip st to first sc, finish off.

EBB AND FLOW

The undulating stripes in this maritime throw bring to mind the soft, rhythmic rise and fall of waves alongside a boat. Fashioned in the colors of a summertime lake, the afghan is a breeze to make.

July

Finished Size: 50" x 69"

MATERIALS
Worsted Weight Yarn:
Blue - 25 ounces,
(710 grams, 1,715 yards)
Dk Blue - 24 ounces,
(680 grams, 1,645 yards)
Lt Blue - 17 ounces,
(480 grams, 1,165 yards)
Crochet hook, size H (5.00 mm) **or** size needed for gauge

GAUGE: In pattern, 18 sts and
18 rows = 4³/₄"

Gauge Swatch: 10¹/₂" x 4³/₄"
With Dk Blue, ch 41 **loosely**.
Work same as Afghan Rows 1-18.

STITCH GUIDE

CROSS STITCH (uses next 2 sts)
(abbreviated Cross St)
Skip next st, dc in next st, working **around** dc just made, dc in skipped st.

Note: Each row is worked across length of Afghan.

With Dk Blue, ch 261 **loosely**.
Row 1 (Right side)**:** Sc in second ch from hook and in each ch across: 260 sc.
Note: Loop a short piece of yarn around any stitch to mark Row 1 as **right** side.
Row 2: Ch 1, turn; sc in each sc across; finish off.
Row 3: With **right** side facing, join Lt Blue with slip st in first sc; ch 3 **(counts as first dc, now and throughout)**, work 2 Cross Sts, sc in next 10 sc, ★ work 5 Cross Sts, sc in next 10 sc; repeat from ★ across to last 5 sc, work 2 Cross Sts, dc in last sc: 64 Cross Sts.
Row 4: Ch 3, turn; work 2 Cross Sts, sc in next 10 sc, ★ work 5 Cross Sts, sc in next 10 sc; repeat from ★ across to last 5 dc, work 2 Cross Sts, dc in last dc; finish off.
Row 5: With **right** side facing, join Dk Blue with slip st in first dc; ch 1, sc in same st and in each st across: 260 sc.
Row 6: Ch 1, turn; sc in each sc across; finish off.
Row 7: With **right** side facing, join Blue with slip st in first sc; ch 1, sc in same st and in next 4 sc, dc in next 10 sc, ★ sc in next 10 sc, dc in next 10 sc; repeat from ★ across to last 5 sc, sc in last 5 sc.
Row 8: Ch 1, turn; sc in first 5 sc, dc in next 10 dc, ★ sc in next 10 sc, dc in next 10 dc; repeat from ★ across to last 5 sc, sc in last 5 sc; finish off.
Row 9: With **right** side facing, join Dk Blue with slip st in first sc; ch 1, sc in same st and in each st across.
Row 10: Ch 1, turn; sc in each sc across; finish off.
Repeat Rows 3-10 until Afghan measures approximately 50" from beginning ch, ending by working Row 6 or Row 10.

Holding 3 strands of Blue together, add fringe evenly across short edges of Afghan *(Figs. 31b & d, page 143)*.

LIBERTY

Our patriotic enthusiasm shines in this all-American throw! The mile-a-minute wrap gets extra pep from decorative popcorns and a picot edging.

Finished Size: 50" x 63"

MATERIALS

Worsted Weight Yarn:

Tan - 31 ounces, (880 grams, 1,950 yards)
Blue - 21 ounces, (600 grams, 1,320 yards)
Red - 20 ounces, (570 grams, 1,255 yards)
Crochet hook, size H (5.00 mm) **or** size needed
for gauge
Yarn needle

GAUGE: Each Strip = 5¹/2" wide

STITCH GUIDE

BEGINNING POPCORN
Ch 3, 4 dc in st or sp indicated, drop loop from hook, insert hook in top of beginning ch-3, hook dropped loop and draw through *(Fig. 20, page 141)*.
POPCORN
5 Dc in st or sp indicated, drop loop from hook, insert hook in first dc of 5-dc group, hook dropped loop and draw through.
BEGINNING V-STITCH (abbreviated V-St)
Ch 4 **(counts as first dc plus ch 1, now and throughout)**, dc in same sp.
V-STITCH (abbreviated V-St)
(Dc, ch 1, dc) in st or sp indicated.
PICOT
Ch 2, slip st in second ch from hook.

STRIP (Make 9)

Foundation Row (Right side)**:** With Tan, ch 3, dc in third ch from hook, (ch 2, dc in top of last dc worked) 81 times: 82 dc and 82 sps.
Note: Loop a short piece of yarn around last dc made to mark Foundation Row as **right** side and bottom edge.

Rnd 1: Slip st **around** post of last dc made, ch 1, 2 sc in same sp, 3 sc around post of each dc across to last dc, 9 sc in last sp, 3 sc in each ch-2 sp across to last ch-2 sp, 7 sc in last ch-2 sp; join with slip st to first sc, finish off: 498 sc.

Rnd 2: With **right** side facing, join Red with slip st in second sc to left of joining; work beginning Popcorn in same st, ch 2, [skip next 2 sc, work Popcorn in next sc, ch 2] 80 times, skip next sc, (work Popcorn in next sc, ch 2) 5 times, (skip next 2 sc, work Popcorn in next sc, ch 2) 81 times, skip next sc, (work Popcorn in next sc, ch 2) 5 times, skip last 2 sc; join with slip st to top of beginning Popcorn, finish off: 172 ch-2 sps.

Rnd 3: With **right** side facing, join Tan with slip st in first ch-2 sp to right of joining; work beginning V-St, work V-St in next 81 ch-2 sps, † work 2 V-Sts in next ch-2 sp, work V-St in next ch-2 sp, work V-St in next Popcorn and in next ch-2 sp, work 2 V-Sts in next ch-2 sp †, work V-St in next 82 ch-2 sps, repeat from † to † once; join with slip st to first dc, finish off: 178 V-Sts.

Rnd 4: With **right** side facing, join Blue with slip st in first V-St (ch-1 sp) to left of joining; work beginning Popcorn in same sp, ch 2, (work Popcorn in next V-St, ch 2) around; join with slip st to top of beginning Popcorn, finish off.

Rnd 5: With **right** side facing, join Tan with slip st in first ch-2 sp to right of joining; work beginning V-St, work V-St in next 82 ch-2 sps, † work 2 V-Sts in each of next 2 ch-2 sps, work V-St in next ch-2 sp, work V-St in next Popcorn and in next ch-2 sp, work 2 V-Sts in each of next 2 ch-2 sps †, work V-St in next 83 ch-2 sps, repeat from † to † once; join with slip st to first dc: 188 V-Sts.

Rnd 6: Ch 1, sc in same st, place marker around sc just made for joining placement, working in each dc and in each ch-1 sp around, sc in each st across to next 2 V-St group, place marker around last sc made for joining placement, sc in next 34 sts, place marker around last sc made for joining placement, sc in each st across to next 2 V-St group, place marker around last sc made for joining placement, sc in last 33 sts; join with slip st to first sc, finish off: 564 sc.

Continued on page 87.

CHEERY GARDEN

The soft palette used to crochet this cheery wrap indulges our innate desire to be pampered. Not only does it capture summer's golden rays and clear blue skies, but it also honors the pretty flowers that abound in July.

Finished Size: 46" x 69"

MATERIALS
Worsted Weight Yarn:
Yellow - 18 ounces, (510 grams, 1,185 yards)
Blue - 16 ounces, (450 grams, 1,055 yards)
Ecru - 13 ounces, (370 grams, 855 yards)
Crochet hook, size I (5.50 mm) **or** size needed for gauge
Yarn needle

GAUGE: Each Square = 5³/4"

Gauge Swatch: 3"
Work same as Square Rnds 1-5.

SQUARE (Make 77)

Rnd 1 (Right side): With Yellow, ch 2, 8 sc in second ch from hook; join with slip st to first sc.
Note: Loop a short piece of yarn around any stitch to mark Rnd 1 as **right** side.
Rnd 2: Ch 1, 2 sc in same st and in each sc around; join with slip st to Front Loop Only of first sc *(Fig. 25, page 142)*, finish off: 16 sc.
Rnd 3: With **right** side facing and working in Front Loops Only, join Blue with slip st in first sc; (ch 5, slip st) in same st **(Petal made)**, ch 5, slip st in next sc, ch 5, ★ (slip st, ch 5) twice in next sc, slip st in next sc, ch 5; repeat from ★ around; join with slip st to first slip st, finish off: 24 Petals.
Rnd 4: With **right** side facing and working in free loops on Rnd 2 *(Fig. 26a, page 142)*, join Ecru with sc in any sc *(see Joining With Sc, page 142)*; 2 sc in next sc, (sc in next sc, 2 sc in next sc) around; join with slip st to **both** loops of first sc: 24 sc.
Rnd 5: Ch 1, working in both loops, sc in same st, ch 1, skip next sc, hdc in next sc, (dc, ch 3, dc) in next sc, hdc in next sc, ch 1, skip next sc, ★ sc in next sc, ch 1, skip next sc, hdc in next sc, (dc, ch 3, dc) in next sc, hdc in next sc, ch 1, skip next sc; repeat from ★ around; join with slip st to first sc: 12 sps.

Rnd 6: Ch 3 **(counts as first dc, now and throughout)**, 2 dc in same st, ch 1, (3 dc, ch 3, 3 dc) in next ch-3 sp, ch 1, ★ 3 dc in next sc, ch 1, (3 dc, ch 3, 3 dc) in next ch-3 sp, ch 1; repeat from ★ around; join with slip st to first dc, finish off.
Rnd 7: With **right** side facing, join Blue with slip st in any ch-3 sp; ch 3, (2 dc, ch 3, 3 dc) in same sp, ch 1, (3 dc in next ch-1 sp, ch 1) across to next ch-3 sp, ★ (3 dc, ch 3, 3 dc) in ch-3 sp, ch 1, (3 dc in next ch-1 sp, ch 1) across to next ch-3 sp; repeat from ★ around; join with slip st to first dc, finish off: 16 sps.
Rnd 8: With Yellow, repeat Rnd 7: 20 sps.

ASSEMBLY

With Yellow and working through both loops, whipstitch Squares together *(Fig. 30b, page 143)*, forming 7 vertical strips of 11 Squares each, beginning in center ch of first corner ch-3 and ending in center ch of next corner ch-3; whipstitch strips together in same manner.

EDGING

Rnd 1: With **right** side facing, join Yellow with sc in any corner ch-3 sp; ch 2, sc in same sp, ★ † ch 1, skip next dc, sc in next dc, ch 1, (sc in next ch-1 sp, ch 1, skip next dc, sc in next dc, ch 1) 4 times, [(sc in next sp, ch 1) twice, skip next dc, sc in next dc, ch 1, (sc in next ch-1 sp, ch 1, skip next dc, sc in next dc, ch 1) 4 times] across to next corner ch-3 sp †, (sc, ch 2, sc) in corner ch-3 sp; repeat from ★ 2 times **more**, then repeat from † to † once; join with slip st to first sc: 396 sps.
Rnd 2: Slip st in first corner ch-2 sp, ch 1, (sc, ch 2, sc) in same sp, ch 1, (sc in next ch-1 sp, ch 1) across to next corner ch-2 sp, ★ (sc, ch 2, sc) in corner ch-2 sp, ch 1, (sc in next ch-1 sp, ch 1) across to next corner ch-2 sp; repeat from ★ around; join with slip st to first sc, finish off: 400 sps.
Rnd 3: With **right** side facing, join Blue with slip st in any corner ch-2 sp; ch 3, (2 dc, ch 3, 3 dc) in same sp, ch 1, skip next ch-1 sp, (3 dc in next ch-1 sp, ch 1, skip next ch-1 sp) across to next corner ch-2 sp, ★ (3 dc, ch 3, 3 dc) in corner ch-2 sp, ch 1, skip next ch-1 sp, (3 dc in next ch-1 sp, ch 1, skip next ch-1 sp) across to next corner ch-2 sp; repeat from ★ around; join with slip st to first dc, finish off.

Continued on page 87.

SUMMER SHERBET

...ed in squares using peach and cream yarns, this lusciou...s wrap has the "flavor" of orange sherbet! A variety of front post clusters give the throw tempting texture.

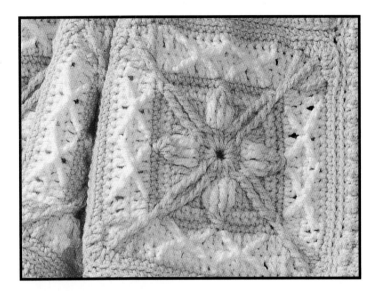

Finished Size: 48" x 63"

MATERIALS
Worsted Weight Yarn:
Peach - 42 ounces, (1,190 grams, 2,450 yards)
Off-White - 29 ounces, (820 grams, 1,690 yards)
Crochet hook, size H (5.00 mm) **or** size needed for gauge
Yarn needle

GAUGE: Each Square = $7\frac{1}{2}$"

Gauge Swatch: $3\frac{1}{4}$"
Work same as Square through Rnd 2.

STITCH GUIDE

TREBLE CROCHET CLUSTER
(abbreviated tr Cluster) (uses next 4 dc)
Working in **front** of tr on Rnd 2, ★ YO twice, insert hook in **next** skipped dc on Rnd 1, YO and pull up a loop, (YO and draw through 2 loops on hook) twice; repeat from ★ 3 times **more**, YO and draw through all 5 loops on hook *(Fig. 15b, page 140)*.

FRONT POST DOUBLE CROCHET CLUSTER
(abbreviated FPdc Cluster)
★ YO, insert hook from **front** to **back** around **next** leg of tr Cluster *(Fig. 16, page 140)*, YO and pull up a loop, YO and draw through 2 loops on hook; repeat from ★ 3 times **more**, YO and draw through all 5 loops on hook. Skip tr Cluster behind FPdc Cluster.

LONG FRONT POST CLUSTER
(abbreviated LFP Cluster)
YO 5 times, insert hook from **front** to **back** around post of dc **before** corner ch-2 sp on Rnd 1, YO and pull up a loop, (YO and draw through 2 loops on hook) 5 times, YO 5 times, insert hook from **front** to **back** around post of dc **after** same corner ch-2 sp on Rnd 1, YO and pull up a loop, (YO and draw through 2 loops on hook) 5 times, YO and draw through all 3 loops on hook *(Figs. 17a & b, page 140)*.

SPLIT TREBLE CROCHET *(abbreviated Split tr)*
YO twice, working in **front** of last 3 dc made, insert hook from **back** to **front** in free loop just created on Rnd 5, YO and pull up a loop, (YO and draw through 2 loops on hook) twice, YO twice, skip next 2 sc, insert hook from **front** to **back** in Front Loop Only of next sc, YO and pull up a loop, (YO and draw through 2 loops on hook) twice, YO and draw through all 3 loops on hook *(Figs. 18a & b, page 140)*.

SPLIT TREBLE CROCHET CLUSTER
(abbreviated Split tr Cluster)
YO twice, working in **front** of last 3 dc made, insert hook from **back** to **front** in center of same Split tr as last tr made, YO and pull up a loop, (YO and draw through 2 loops on hook) twice, YO twice, skip next 3 dc, insert hook from **front** to **back** in center of next Split tr, YO and pull up a loop, (YO and draw through 2 loops on hook) twice, YO and draw through all 3 loops on hook *(Figs. 19a & b, page 140)*.

FRONT POST DOUBLE TREBLE CROCHET
(abbreviated FPdtr)
YO 3 times, insert hook from **front** to **back** around post of center dc of corner 3-dc group on Rnd 6 *(Fig. 13, page 139)*, YO and pull up a loop, (YO and draw through 2 loops on hook) 4 times.

Continued on page 86.

SQUARE (Make 48)

With Peach, ch 4; join with slip st to form a ring.

Rnd 1 (Right side)**:** Ch 3 **(counts as first dc, now and throughout)**, 3 dc in ring, (ch 2, 4 dc in ring) 3 times, hdc in first dc to form last ch-2 sp: 16 dc and 4 ch-2 sps.

Note: Loop a short piece of yarn around any stitch to mark Rnd 1 as **right** side.

Rnd 2: Ch 4 **(counts as first tr)**, 8 tr in same sp, skip next 4 dc, (9 tr in next ch-2 sp, skip next 4 dc) 3 times; join with slip st to first tr, finish off: 36 tr.

Rnd 3: With **right** side facing, join Off-White with sc in center tr of any 9-tr group *(see Joining With Sc, page 142)*; 2 sc in same st, sc in next 4 tr, work tr Cluster, sc in next 4 tr, ★ 3 sc in next tr, sc in next 4 tr, work tr Cluster, sc in next 4 tr; repeat from ★ around; join with slip st to first sc, finish off: 44 sc and 4 tr Clusters.

Rnd 4: With **right** side facing, join Peach with sc in third sc of any corner 3-sc group; sc in next 4 sc, work FPdc Cluster, sc in next 6 sc, work LFP Cluster, ★ sc in same st as last sc and in next 5 sc, work FPdc Cluster, sc in next 6 sc, work LFP Cluster; repeat from ★ around, sc in same st as last sc; join with slip st to first sc: 48 sc.

Rnd 5: Ch 1, sc in same st and in next 4 sc, skip next FPdc Cluster, sc in next 6 sc, 3 sc in next LFP Cluster, ★ sc in next 6 sc, skip next FPdc Cluster, sc in next 6 sc, 3 sc in next LFP Cluster; repeat from ★ around to last sc, sc in last sc; join with slip st to first sc, finish off: 60 sc.

Rnd 6: With **right** side facing, join Off-White with slip st in center sc of any corner 3-sc group; ch 3, 2 dc in same st, ★ † dc in **both** loops of next sc, [dc in Back Loop Only of next sc *(Fig. 25, page 142)*, dc in **both** loops of next 2 sc, work Split tr, working **behind** Split tr just made, dc in **both** loops of 2 skipped sc, dc in free loop of next sc *(Fig. 26a, page 142)*] twice, dc in **both** loops of next sc †, 3 dc in next sc; repeat from ★ 2 times **more**, then repeat from † to † once; join with slip st to first dc: 68 dc and 8 Split tr.

Rnd 7: Ch 3, 3 tr in next dc, ★ † dc in next 2 dc, skip next 3 dc, tr in center of next Split tr *(Fig. 1)*; working **behind** tr just made, dc in 3 skipped dc, skip next Split tr, dc in next 3 dc, work Split tr Cluster, working **behind** Split tr Cluster just made, dc in 3 skipped dc, skip next Split tr, dc in next 3 dc, working in **front** of last 3 dc made and inserting hook from **back** to **front**, tr in center of same Split tr as last Split tr Cluster †, dc in next 2 dc, 3 tr in next dc; repeat from ★ 2 times **more**, then repeat from † to † once, dc in last dc; join with slip st to first dc, finish off: 64 dc and 20 tr.

Fig. 1

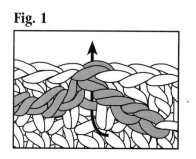

Rnd 8: With **right** side facing, join Peach with sc in center tr of any corner 3-tr group; ★ † YO 5 times, insert hook from **front** to **back** around **both** posts of LFP Cluster on Rnd 4, YO and pull up a loop, (YO and draw through 2 loops on hook) 6 times, sc in same st as last sc made and in next tr, work FPdtr, sc in dc **behind** FPdtr and in next 18 sts, work FPdtr †, sc in tr **behind** FPdtr and in next tr; repeat from ★ 2 times **more**, then repeat from † to † once, sc in last tr **behind** FPdtr; join with slip st to first sc: 92 sc.

Rnd 9: Ch 3, 3 dc in next st, dc in next 2 sc, hdc in next FPdtr, sc in next 19 sc, hdc in next FPdtr, ★ dc in next 2 sc, 3 dc in next st, dc in next 2 sc, hdc in next FPdtr, sc in next 19 sc, hdc in next FPdtr; repeat from ★ around to last sc, dc in last sc; join with slip st to first dc, finish off: 112 sts.

ASSEMBLY

With Peach and working through inside loops only, whipstitch Squares together *(Fig. 30a, page 143)*, forming 6 vertical strips of 8 Squares each, beginning in center dc of first corner and ending in center dc of next corner; whipstitch strips together in same manner.

EDGING

Rnd 1: With **right** side facing and working in Back Loops Only, join Peach with sc in center dc of any corner 3-dc group; 2 sc in same st, ★ † sc in next 27 sts, (sc in same st as joining on same Square and in same st as joining on next Square, sc in next 27 sts) across to center dc of next corner 3-dc group †, 3 sc in center dc; repeat from ★ 2 times **more**, then repeat from † to † once; join with slip st to Back Loop Only of first sc, finish off: 816 sc.

Rnd 2: With **right** side facing and working in Back Loops Only, join Off-White with sc in center sc of any corner 3-sc group; 2 sc in same st and in next sc, sc in each sc across to center sc of next corner 3-sc group, ★ 3 sc in center sc, 2 sc in next sc, sc in each sc across to center sc of next corner 3-sc group; repeat from ★ around; join with slip st to **both** loops of first sc, finish off: 828 sc.

Note: Push tr to **right** side of Afghan.

Rnd 3: With **right** side facing and working in both loops, join Peach with sc in center sc of any corner 3-sc group; 2 sc in same st, tr in next sc, (sc in next sc, tr in next sc) across to center sc of next corner 3-sc group, ★ 3 sc in center sc, tr in next sc, (sc in next sc, tr in next sc) across to center sc of next corner 3-sc group; repeat from ★ around; join with slip st to first sc: 836 sts.

Rnd 4: Ch 3, 3 dc in next sc, dc in each st around working 3 dc in center sc of each corner 3-sc group; join with slip st to first dc, finish off.

LIBERTY Continued from page 80.

ASSEMBLY

Place two Strips with **wrong** sides together and bottom edges at same end. With Tan and working through inside loops only, whipstitch Strips together *(Fig. 30a, page 143)*, beginning in first marked sc and ending in next marked sc. Do **not** remove markers from outside edge of first Strip.

EDGING

With **right** side facing and working across long side, join Tan with slip st in first marked sc, remove all markers; ch 1, sc in same st and in next sc, work Picot, (skip next sc, sc in next 2 sc, work Picot) 83 times, † [skip next sc, (sc in next 2 sc, work Picot) twice] 5 times, skip next sc, sc in next 2 sc, work Picot, sc in next 2 sc, ★ skip next sc, sc in next 2 sc on next Strip, work Picot, [skip next sc, (sc in next 2 sc, work Picot) twice] 5 times, skip next sc, sc in next 2 sc, work Picot, sc in next 2 sc; repeat from ★ 7 times **more** †, work Picot, (skip next sc, sc in next 2 sc, work Picot) 84 times, repeat from † to † once, skip last sc; join with slip st to first sc, finish off.

CHEERY GARDEN Continued from page 82.

Rnd 4: With **right** side facing, join Ecru with slip st in any corner ch-3 sp; ch 3, (2 dc, ch 3, 3 dc) in same sp, ch 1, (3 dc in next ch-1 sp, ch 1) across to next corner ch-3 sp, ★ (3 dc, ch 3, 3 dc) in corner ch-3 sp, ch 1, (3 dc in next ch-1 sp, ch 1) across to next corner ch-3 sp; repeat from ★ around; join with slip st to first dc, finish off.

Rnd 5: With Blue, repeat Rnd 4.

Rnd 6: With Yellow, repeat Rnd 4; do **not** finish off.

Rnd 7: Slip st in next dc, ch 1, sc in same st, ch 1, (sc, ch 2, sc) in next corner ch-3 sp, ★ ch 1, skip next dc, sc in next dc, ch 1, (sc in next ch-1 sp, ch 1, skip next dc, sc in next dc, ch 1) across to next corner ch-3 sp, (sc, ch 2, sc) in corner ch-3 sp; repeat from ★ 2 times **more**, ch 1, skip next dc, (sc in next dc, ch 1, sc in next ch-1 sp, ch 1, skip next dc) across; join with slip st to first sc.

Rnd 8: Slip st in first ch-1 sp, ch 1, (slip st, ch 1) twice in next corner ch-2 sp, ★ (slip st in next ch-1 sp, ch 1) across to next corner ch-2 sp, (slip st, ch 1) twice in corner ch-2 sp; repeat from ★ 2 times **more**, (slip st in next ch-1 sp, ch 1) across; join with slip st to first slip st, finish off.

NATURAL STRIPES

Quick to make holding two strands of yarn, this plush throw is fashioned in deep, woodsy tones that form natural stripes. Long double crochets create the teardrop effect, while fringe continues the flowing look.

Finished Size: 45" x 61"

MATERIALS
Worsted Weight Yarn:
Green - 17 ounces,
    (480 grams, 1,115 yards)
Dk Green - 14 ounces,
    (400 grams, 920 yards)
Ecru - 14 ounces,
    (400 grams, 920 yards)
Crochet hook, size Q (15.00 mm)

Note: Entire Afghan is worked holding two strands of yarn together.

GAUGE: 12 sc = 8"; 10 rows = 5½"

Gauge Swatch: 7½" x 5½"
Ch 12 **loosely.**
Work same as Afghan for 10 rows.
Finish off.

STITCH GUIDE

LONG DOUBLE CROCHET (abbreviated LDC)
Working **around** next sc, dc in sc one row **below** next sc **(Fig. 22, page 141)**.

COLOR SEQUENCE
2 Rows **each:** Green **(Fig. 27a, page 142)**, ★ Dk Green, Ecru, Green; repeat from ★ throughout.

With Green, ch 68 **loosely.**
Row 1 (Right side)**:** Sc in second ch from hook and in each ch across: 67 sc.
Note: Loop a short piece of yarn around any stitch to mark Row 1 as **right** side.
Row 2: Ch 1, turn; sc in each sc across, changing colors in last sc.
Row 3: Ch 1, turn; sc in first sc, work LDC, (sc in next 3 sc, work LDC) across to last sc, sc in last sc: 17 LDC.
Row 4: Ch 1, turn; sc in each st across, changing colors in last sc.
Row 5: Ch 1, turn; sc in first 3 sc, (work LDC, sc in next 3 sc) across.
Row 6: Ch 1, turn; sc in each st across, changing colors in last sc.
Repeat Rows 3-6 until Afghan measures approximately 61" from beginning ch, ending by working 2 rows Green and Row 6; do **not** change colors, finish off.

Holding 4 strands of Green together, add fringe evenly across short edges of Afghan **(Figs. 31a & c, page 143)**.

89

SOOTHING WAVES

Like whitecapped waves that soothe our souls, this nautical comforter offers us quiet serenity. The blue and ecru "waves" are formed with simple shells.

Finished Size: 51¹/₂" x 59"

MATERIALS
Worsted Weight Yarn:
    Ecru - 15 ounces, (430 grams, 1,030 yards)
    Lt Blue - 12 ounces, (340 grams, 825 yards)
    Blue - 12 ounces, (340 grams, 825 yards)
Crochet hook, size H (5.00 mm) **or** size needed
    for gauge

GAUGE SWATCH: 5¹/₄" x 3¹/₂"
Ch 20 **loosely**.
Work same as Afghan for 8 rows.
Finish off.

STITCH GUIDE

> **SHELL**
> Dc in st indicated, (ch 1, dc) twice in same st.

AFGHAN BODY

With Ecru, ch 182 **loosely**.
Row 1 (Right side)**:** Sc in second ch from hook, ★ ch 1, skip next 2 chs, work Shell in next ch, ch 1, skip next 2 chs, sc in next ch; repeat from ★ across; finish off: 30 Shells and 31 sc.
Note: Loop a short piece of yarn around any stitch to mark Row 1 as **right** side.

Row 2: With **wrong** side facing, join Lt Blue with slip st in first sc; ch 5 **(counts as first dc plus ch 2)**, skip next dc, sc in next dc, ch 2, skip next dc, dc in next sc, ★ ch 2, skip next dc, sc in next dc, ch 2, skip next dc, dc in next sc; repeat from ★ across: 31 dc and 30 sc.
Row 3: Ch 1, turn; sc in first dc, ★ ch 1, work Shell in next sc, ch 1, sc in next dc; repeat from ★ across; finish off: 30 Shells and 31 sc.
Rows 4 and 5: With Blue, repeat Rows 2 and 3.
Rows 6 and 7: With Ecru, repeat Rows 2 and 3.
Repeat Rows 2-7 until Afghan measures approximately 57¹/₂" from beginning ch, ending by working Row 6; do **not** finish off.

EDGING

Rnd 1: Ch 1, turn; slip st in first dc, ch 2, skip next ch-2 sp, (slip st in next st, ch 2, skip next ch-2 sp) across to last dc, (slip st, ch 3, slip st) in last dc, ch 2; working in end of rows, (slip st in next row, ch 2, skip next row) across; working in free loops of beginning ch *(Fig. 26b, page 142)*, (slip st, ch 3, slip st) in first ch, (ch 2, skip next 2 chs, slip st in next ch) 59 times, ch 2, skip next 2 chs, (slip st, ch 3, slip st) in next ch; working in end of rows, ch 2, skip first row, slip st in next row, (ch 2, skip next row, slip st in next row) across, ch 2, slip st in same st as first slip st, ch 3; join with slip st to first slip st.
Rnd 2: Slip st in first ch-2 sp, ch 1, sc in same sp, ch 2, ★ (sc in next ch-2 sp, ch 2) across to next corner ch-3 sp, (sc, ch 2) twice in corner ch-3 sp; repeat from ★ around; join with slip st to first sc.
Rnd 3: (Slip st, ch 2, dc) in each ch-2 sp around; join with slip st to first slip st, finish off.

FREEDOM DAY

Bold and beautiful, this spirited wrap honors our great country. Though the afghan sports a pattern of colorful squares, it's actually crocheted in strips.

Finished Size: 54" x 72"

MATERIALS
Worsted Weight Yarn:
　Blue - 43 ounces, (1,220 grams, 2,950 yards)
　Tan - 19 ounces, (540 grams, 1,305 yards)
　Red - 19 ounces, (540 grams, 1,305 yards)
Crochet hook, size I (5.50 mm) **or** size needed
　for gauge
Yarn needle

GAUGE: In pattern, 20 sts = 6"; 12 rows = 5¹/₂"
　　　　　Each Strip = 6" wide

Gauge Swatch: 6"w x 5¹/₂"h
Work same as Strip A through Row 12.

STRIP A (Make 5)
COLOR SEQUENCE
12 Rows Blue *(Fig. 27a, page 142)*, ★ (2 rows Red, 2 rows Ecru) 3 times, 12 rows Blue; repeat from ★ 5 times **more**.

With Blue, ch 21 **loosely**.
Row 1: Sc in second ch from hook, skip next 3 chs, (tr, 3 dc) in next ch, ★ ch 2, sc in next ch, skip next 3 chs, (tr, 3 dc) in next ch; repeat from ★ across: 20 sts and 3 ch-2 sps.
Row 2 (Right side)**:** Ch 1, turn; sc in first dc, skip next 3 sts, (tr, 3 dc) in next sc, ★ ch 2, sc in next ch-2 sp, skip next 4 sts, (tr, 3 dc) in next sc; repeat from ★ across.
Note: Loop a short piece of yarn around any stitch to mark Row 2 as **right** side and bottom edge.
Rows 3-156: Ch 1, turn; sc in first dc, skip next 3 sts, (tr, 3 dc) in next sc, ★ ch 2, sc in next ch-2 sp, skip next 4 sts, (tr, 3 dc) in next sc; repeat from ★ across.
Finish off.

STRIP B (Make 4)
COLOR SEQUENCE
(2 Rows Red, 2 rows Ecru) 3 times, ★ 12 rows Blue, (2 rows Red, 2 rows Ecru) 3 times; repeat from ★ 5 times **more**.

With Red, ch 21 **loosely**.
Row 1: Sc in second ch from hook, skip next 3 chs, (tr, 3 dc) in next ch, ★ ch 2, sc in next ch, skip next 3 chs, (tr, 3 dc) in next ch; repeat from ★ across: 20 sts and 3 ch-2 sps.
Row 2 (Right side)**:** Ch 1, turn; sc in first dc, skip next 3 sts, (tr, 3 dc) in next sc, ★ ch 2, sc in next ch-2 sp, skip next 4 sts, (tr, 3 dc) in next sc; repeat from ★ across.
Note: Mark Row 2 as **right** side and bottom edge.
Rows 3-156: Ch 1, turn; sc in first dc, skip next 3 sts, (tr, 3 dc) in next sc, ★ ch 2, sc in next ch-2 sp, skip next 4 sts, (tr, 3 dc) in next sc; repeat from ★ across.
Finish off.

ASSEMBLY
Afghan is assembled by joining Strips in following sequence: Strip A, (Strip B, Strip A) 4 times.

Place two Strips with **right** sides together and bottom edges at same end; with Blue, sew through both pieces once to secure the beginning of the seam, leaving an ample yarn end to weave in later. Insert the needle from **back** to **front** through one strand on each piece *(Fig. 1)*. Bring the needle around and insert it from **back** to **front** through the next strand on both pieces.
Repeat along the edge, being careful to match rows.

Fig. 1

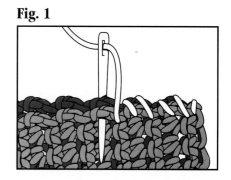

Holding 10 strands of Blue together, add fringe evenly across short edges of Afghan *(Figs. 31a & c, page 143)*.

COZY RIPPLE

Create a cozy coverlet for the bedroom by crocheting this wrap in a shade that complements your linens. The decorative pattern is simple to make and offers lots of warmth and classic style.

Finished Size: 47" x 64"

MATERIALS
Worsted Weight Yarn:
    49 ounces, (1,390 grams, 3,105 yards)
Crochet hook, size I (5.50 mm) **or** size needed
    for gauge

GAUGE: Each repeat from point to point and
    7 rows = 4¼"

Gauge Swatch: 8½"w x 4¼"h
Ch 37 **loosely**.
Work same as Afghan for 7 rows.
Finish off.

STITCH GUIDE

DECREASE (uses next 3 sts)
★ YO, insert hook in **next** st, YO and pull up a loop, YO and draw through 2 loops on hook; repeat from ★ 2 times **more**, YO and draw through all 4 loops on hook **(counts as one dc)**.

ENDING DECREASE (uses last 3 dc)
YO, insert hook in next dc, YO and pull up a loop, YO and draw through 2 loops on hook, YO, skip next dc, insert hook in last dc, YO and pull up a loop, YO and draw through 2 loops on hook, YO and draw through all 3 loops on hook **(counts as one dc)**.

CLUSTER (uses next 3 dc)
YO, insert hook in next dc, YO and pull up a loop, YO and draw through 2 loops on hook, YO twice, insert hook in next dc, YO and pull up a loop, (YO and draw through 2 loops on hook) twice, ★ YO twice, insert hook in **same** dc, YO and pull up a loop, (YO and draw through 2 loops on hook) twice; repeat from ★ 2 times **more**, YO, insert hook in next dc, YO and pull up a loop, YO and draw through 2 loops on hook, YO and draw through all 7 loops on hook *(Fig. 15b, page 140)*.
Push Cluster to **right** side.

Ch 190 **loosely**.
Row 1 (Right side)**:** Dc in fourth ch from hook **(3 skipped chs count as first dc)** and in next 7 chs, ch 2, dc in next 7 chs, ★ decrease, dc in next 7 chs, ch 2, dc in next 7 chs; repeat from ★ across to last 2 chs, [(YO, insert hook in **next** ch, YO and pull up a loop, YO and draw through 2 loops on hook) twice, YO and draw through all 3 loops on hook **(counts as one dc)**]: 167 dc and 11 ch-2 sps.
Row 2: Ch 3 **(counts as first dc, now and throughout)**, turn; dc in next 6 dc, ch 1, skip next dc, dc in next ch, ch 2, dc in next ch, ch 1, skip next dc, dc in next 5 dc, ★ work Cluster, dc in next 5 dc, ch 1, skip next dc, dc in next ch, ch 2, dc in next ch, ch 1, skip next dc, dc in next 5 dc; repeat from ★ across to last 3 dc, work ending decrease: 135 dc, 10 Clusters, and 33 sps.
Row 3: Ch 3, turn; dc in next 4 dc, (ch 1, skip next dc, dc in next ch) twice, ch 2, (dc in next ch, ch 1, skip next dc) twice, dc in next 3 dc, ★ decrease, dc in next 3 dc, (ch 1, skip next dc, dc in next ch) twice, ch 2, (dc in next ch, ch 1, skip next dc) twice, dc in next 3 dc; repeat from ★ across to last 3 dc, work ending decrease: 123 dc and 55 sps.
Row 4: Ch 3, turn; dc in next 2 dc, (ch 1, skip next dc, dc in next ch) 3 times, ch 2, (dc in next ch, ch 1, skip next dc) 3 times, dc in next dc, ★ work Cluster, dc in next dc, (ch 1, skip next dc, dc in next ch) 3 times, ch 2, (dc in next ch, ch 1, skip next dc) 3 times, dc in next dc; repeat from ★ across to last 3 dc, work ending decrease: 91 dc, 10 Clusters, and 77 sps.
Row 5: Ch 3, turn; (dc in next dc and in next ch) 4 times, ch 2, dc in next ch, (dc in next dc and in next ch) 3 times, ★ decrease, dc in next ch, (dc in next dc and in next ch) 3 times, ch 2, dc in next ch, (dc in next dc and in next ch) 3 times; repeat from ★ across to last 3 dc, work ending decrease: 167 dc and 11 ch-2 sps.
Repeat Rows 2-5, until Afghan measures approximately 64" from beginning ch at point, ending by working Row 5; do **not** finish off.

Edging: Ch 2, do **not** turn; working in end of rows, skip first row, (slip st in top of next row, ch 2) across; working in free loops of beginning ch *(Fig. 26b, page 142)*, (slip st, ch 1, slip st) in first ch, ★ ch 1, skip next ch, (slip st in next ch, ch 1, skip next ch) 3 times, slip st in next 2 chs, ch 1, skip next ch, (slip st in next ch, ch 1, skip next ch) 3 times, (slip st, ch 1, slip st) in next ch; repeat from ★ across, ch 2; working in end of rows, slip st in top of first row, ch 2, (slip st in top of next row, ch 2) across to last row, skip last row; working in sts on Row 105, slip st in first 2 dc, ch 1, skip next dc, (slip st in next dc, ch 1, skip next dc) 3 times, (slip st, ch 1) twice in next ch-2 sp, † skip next dc, (slip st in next st, ch 1, skip next dc) 7 times, (slip st, ch 1) twice in next ch-2 sp †, repeat from † to † across to last 8 dc, skip next dc, slip st in next dc, (ch 1, skip next dc, slip st in next dc) across; join with slip st to base of beginning ch-2, finish off.

FRUITED PLAINS

The subtle texture of this handsome throw has rich visual impact.
The rows are worked in shades of green across the length of the afghan.

Finished Size: 51" x 70½"

MATERIALS
 Worsted Weight Yarn:
  Lt Green - 39 ounces,
   (1,110 grams, 2,565 yards)
  Green - 17 ounces,
   (480 grams, 1,115 yards)
 Crochet hook, size I (5.50 mm) **or** size
  needed for gauge

GAUGE: In pattern, 15 sts and
   15 rows = 4"

Gauge Swatch: 4½"w x 4"h
Ch 18 **loosely**.
Work same as Afghan Rows 1-15.

COLOR SEQUENCE
(One row Lt Green, one row Green) 4 times, ★ 7 rows Lt Green, one row Green, (one row Lt Green, one row Green) 3 times; repeat from ★ 12 times **more**, then work one row Lt Green.

Note: Each row is worked across length of Afghan. When joining yarn and finishing off, always leave a 9" end to be worked into fringe.

AFGHAN BODY
With Lt Green, ch 264 **loosely**.
Row 1 (Wrong side)**:** Sc in second ch from hook, (ch 1, skip next ch, sc in next ch) across; finish off: 132 sc.
Note: Loop a short piece of yarn around the **back** of any stitch to mark **right** side.
Row 2: With **right** side facing, join yarn with sc in first sc *(see Joining With Sc, page 142)*; (ch 1, sc in next sc) across; finish off.
Row 3: With **wrong** side facing, join yarn with sc in first sc; (ch 1, sc in next sc) across; finish off.
Row 4: With **right** side facing, join yarn with sc in first sc; skip next ch-1 sp and next sc, working in **front** of previous rows, tr in ch-1 sp 2 rows **below** next ch-1, sc in skipped sc, ★ (ch 1, sc in next sc) twice, skip next ch-1 sp and next sc, working in **front** of previous rows, tr in ch-1 sp 2 rows **below** next ch-1, sc in skipped sc; repeat from ★ across to last sc, ch 1, sc in last sc; finish off: 44 tr.
Row 5: With **wrong** side facing, join yarn with sc in first sc; ch 1, skip next ch, sc in next sc, ch 1, skip next tr, sc in next sc, ★ (ch 1, skip next ch, sc in next sc) twice, ch 1, skip next tr, sc in next sc; repeat from ★ across; finish off: 132 sc.
Repeat Rows 4 and 5, until Afghan measures approximately 51" from beginning ch, ending by working Row 5.

EDGING
FIRST SIDE
With **right** side facing, join Lt Green with slip st in first sc; slip st in next ch-1 sp, (ch 1, slip st in next ch-1 sp) across to last sc, slip st in last sc; finish off.

SECOND SIDE
With **right** side facing, join Lt Green with slip st in free loop of ch at base of first sc *(Fig. 26b, page 142)*; working over beginning ch, slip st in next ch-1 sp, (ch 1, skip next ch, slip st in next ch-1 sp) across to last ch, slip st in free loop of last ch; finish off.

Holding 3 strands of corresponding color together, add additional fringe evenly across short edges of Afghan *(Figs. 31b & d, page 143)*.

COUNTRY PLEASURES

Hidden among the ripples of this inviting afghan is a charming flower garden! Created with front post clusters, the "flowers" echo the deep hues of the wrap. Fringe on the peaks of the afghan provides a nice finish.

Finished Size: 50" x 66"

MATERIALS

Worsted Weight Yarn:

Rose - 27 ounces, (770 grams, 1,850 yards)

Green - 19 ounces, (540 grams, 1,305 yards)

Ecru - 12¹/₂ ounces, (360 grams, 860 yards)

Crochet hook, size G (4.00 mm) **or** size needed for gauge

GAUGE: Each repeat from point to point = 4¹/₂";
7 rows = 3³/₄"

Gauge Swatch: 9"w x 3³/₄"h

With Green, ch 40 **loosely**.

Work same as Afghan for 7 rows.

Finish off.

STITCH GUIDE

DECREASE (uses last 2 dc)

★ YO, insert hook in **next** dc, YO and pull up a loop, YO and draw through 2 loops on hook; repeat from ★ once **more**, YO and draw through all 3 loops on hook (**counts as one dc**).

FRONT POST CLUSTER (*abbreviated FP Cluster*)

Working in **front** of dc indicated, YO 3 times, insert hook from **front** to **back** around post of dc one row **below** dc (*Fig. 9, page 139*), YO and pull up a loop, (YO and draw through 2 loops on hook) 3 times, ★ working in **front** of same dc, YO 3 times, insert hook from **front** to **back** around post of **same** dc one row **below** dc, YO and pull up a loop, (YO and draw through 2 loops on hook) 3 times; repeat from ★ once **more**, YO and draw through all 4 loops on hook.

With Green, ch 211 **loosely**.

Row 1 (Right side)**:** Dc in fifth ch from hook (**4 skipped chs count as first dc plus one skipped ch**) and in next 6 chs, 3 dc in next ch, ★ dc in next 8 chs, skip next 2 chs, dc in next 8 chs, 3 dc in next ch; repeat from ★ across to last 9 chs, dc in next 7 chs, skip next ch, dc in last ch: 209 dc.

Note: Loop a short piece of yarn around any stitch to mark Row 1 as **right** side.

Row 2: Ch 2, turn; skip next dc, dc in next 7 dc, 3 dc in next dc, ★ dc in next 8 dc, skip next 2 dc, dc in next 8 dc, 3 dc in next dc; repeat from ★ across to last 9 dc, dc in next 6 dc, † YO, insert hook in **next** dc, YO and pull up a loop, YO and draw through 2 loops on hook †, skip next dc, repeat from † to † once, with Ecru YO and draw through all 3 loops on hook (*Fig. 27a, page 142*): 207 dc.

Row 3: Ch 2, turn; dc in next 7 dc, 3 dc in next dc, ★ dc in next 8 dc, skip next 2 dc, dc in next 8 dc, 3 dc in next dc; repeat from ★ across to last 8 dc, dc in next 6 dc, decrease.

Row 4: Ch 2, turn; dc in next 7 dc, 3 dc in next dc, ★ dc in next 8 dc, skip next 2 dc, dc in next 8 dc, 3 dc in next dc; repeat from ★ across to last 8 dc, dc in next 6 dc, decrease changing to Rose.

Row 5: Ch 2, turn; dc in next 5 dc, † working in **front** of next dc, work FP Cluster, skip dc behind FP Cluster, dc in next 2 dc, working in **front** of last dc worked into, work FP Cluster, dc in same st as last dc and in next dc, working in **front** of next dc, work FP Cluster, skip dc behind FP Cluster †, ★ dc in next 6 dc, skip next 2 dc, dc in next 6 dc, repeat from † to † once; repeat from ★ across to last 6 dc, dc in next 4 dc, decrease.

Rows 6 and 7: Ch 2, turn; dc in next 7 sts, 3 dc in next st, ★ dc in next 8 sts, skip next 2 dc, dc in next 8 sts, 3 dc in next st; repeat from ★ across to last 8 sts, dc in next 6 sts, decrease.

Row 8: Ch 2, turn; dc in next 7 dc, 3 dc in next dc, ★ dc in next 8 dc, skip next 2 dc, dc in next 8 dc, 3 dc in next dc; repeat from ★ across to last 8 dc, dc in next 6 dc, decrease changing to Green.

Continued on page 104.

WESTERN AMBIENCE

If you've been trying to round up an afghan for your favorite cowpoke, look no further! This mile-a-minute throw is worked in rust, tan, and turquoise for a Western ambience that's sure to please.

Finished Size: 53" x 66"

MATERIALS
Worsted Weight Yarn:
    Rust - 27 ounces, (770 grams, 1,900 yards)
    Tan - 20 ounces, (570 grams, 1,405 yards)
    Turquoise - 13 ounces, (370 grams, 915 yards)
Crochet hook, size I (5.50 mm) **or** size needed
    for gauge
Yarn needle

GAUGE: Each Strip = 4³/₄" wide

STITCH GUIDE

LONG DOUBLE CROCHET (abbreviated LDC)
YO, insert hook in st or sp indicated, YO and pull up a loop even with loop on hook, (YO and draw through 2 loops on hook) twice *(Fig. 22, page 141)*. Skip st behind LDC.

FRONT POST DOUBLE CROCHET
    (abbreviated FPdc)
YO, insert hook from **front** to **back** around post of st indicated, YO and pull up a loop *(Fig. 11, page 139)*, (YO and draw through 2 loops on hook) twice. Skip st behind FPdc.

FRONT POST SINGLE CROCHET (abbreviated FPsc)
Insert hook from **front** to **back** around post of st indicated, YO and pull up a loop *(Fig. 10, page 139)*, YO and draw through both loops on hook. Skip st behind FPsc.

DECREASE
Insert hook in next sc, YO and pull up a loop, insert hook in same st as joining on same Strip, YO and pull up a loop, insert hook in same st as joining on next Strip, YO and pull up a loop, insert hook in next sc, YO and pull up a loop, YO and draw through all 5 loops on hook.

STRIP (Make 11)

Foundation Row (Right side)**:** With Turquoise, ch 4, tr in fourth ch from hook, (ch 3, tr in top of last tr worked) 55 times: 56 tr and 56 sps.

Note: Loop a short piece of yarn around last tr made to mark Foundation Row as **right** side and bottom edge.

Rnd 1: Slip st **around** post of last tr made, ch 3 **(counts as first dc, now and throughout)**, 3 dc in same sp, 4 dc around post of each tr across to last tr, 16 dc in last sp, 4 dc in each ch-3 sp across to last ch-3 sp, 12 dc in last ch-3 sp; join with slip st to first dc, finish off: 464 dc.

Rnd 2: With **right** side facing, join Tan with slip st in fifth dc to left of joining; ch 1, sc in same st and in next 2 dc, [working **around** previous rnd, work LDC in top of next tr on Foundation Row, sc in next 3 dc] 54 times, † (working **around** previous rnd, work LDC in same sp as next dc on Foundation Row, sc in next 3 dc) 3 times †, [working **around** previous rnd, work LDC in top of next tr (same st as LDC on opposite side), sc in next 3 dc] 55 times, repeat from † to † once, working **around** previous rnd, work LDC in top of next tr (same st as LDC on opposite side); join with slip st to first sc: 116 LDC.

Rnd 3: Ch 3, dc in next 2 sc, work FPdc around next LDC, (dc in next 3 sc, work FPdc around next LDC) 53 times, † (dc in next sc, 2 dc in next sc, dc in next sc, work FPdc around next LDC) 4 times †, (dc in next 3 sc, work FPdc around next LDC) 54 times, repeat from † to † once; join with slip st to first dc, finish off: 356 dc and 116 FPdc.

Rnd 4: With **right** side facing, join Rust with slip st in same st as joining; ch 1, sc in same st and in next 2 dc, (work FPdc around next FPdc, sc in next 3 dc) 54 times, † 2 sc in next dc, work FPdc around next FPdc, 2 sc in next dc, ★ sc in next 2 dc, 2 sc in next dc, work FPdc around next FPdc, 2 sc in next dc; repeat from ★ once **more**, sc in next 3 dc †, (work FPdc around next FPdc, sc in next 3 dc) 55 times, repeat from † to † once, work FPdc around last FPdc; join with slip st in first sc, do **not** finish off: 368 sc and 116 FPdc.

Continued on page 105.

Grand comforts such as this heirloom beauty are not just a thing of the past. The lacy throw is simple to make with mostly double crochet, chain, and puff stitches. For an antique look, we chose creamy ecru.

Finished Size: 46" x 63"

MATERIALS
Worsted Weight Yarn:
   59 ounces, (1,680 grams, 2,850 yards)
Crochet hook, size G (4.00 mm) **or** size needed
   for gauge

GAUGE: In pattern, one repeat = 3";
   8 rows = 4¼"

Gauge Swatch: 5"w x 4¼"h
Ch 24 **loosely**.
Work same as Afghan for 8 rows.
Finish off.

STITCH GUIDE

BEGINNING PUFF STITCH
   (abbreviated beginning Puff St)

Ch 2, ★ YO, insert hook in st or sp indicated, YO and pull up a loop even with loop on hook; repeat from ★ 2 times **more**, YO and draw through all 7 loops on hook *(Fig. 21, page 141)*.

PUFF STITCH *(abbreviated Puff St)*

★ YO, insert hook in st or sp indicated, YO and pull up a loop even with loop on hook; repeat from ★ 3 times **more**, YO and draw through all 9 loops on hook.

PICOT

Ch 3, slip st in top of dc just made.

AFGHAN BODY

Ch 167 **loosely**.

Row 1 (Right side)**:** Dc in fifth ch from hook **(4 skipped chs count as first dc plus one skipped ch)**, ch 1, skip next ch, (2 dc, ch 1) twice in next ch, ★ skip next ch, dc in next ch, ch 2, skip next 3 chs, (work Puff St in next ch, ch 2) twice, skip next 3 chs, dc in next ch, ch 1, skip next ch, (2 dc, ch 1) twice in next ch; repeat from ★ across to last 4 chs, (skip next ch, dc in next ch) twice: 24 Puff Sts, 80 dc, and 75 sps.

Rows 2-104: Ch 3 **(counts as first dc, now and throughout)**, turn; dc in next ch-1 sp, ch 1, (2 dc, ch 1) twice in next ch-1 sp, dc in next ch-1 sp, ★ ch 2, skip next ch-2 sp, (work Puff St, ch 2) twice in next ch-2 sp, skip next ch-2 sp, dc in next ch-1 sp, ch 1, (2 dc, ch 1) twice in next ch-1 sp, dc in next ch-1 sp; repeat from ★ across to last 2 dc, skip next dc, dc in last dc.

Row 105: Ch 3, turn; hdc in next ch-1 sp, ch 1, (sc, ch 2, sc) in next ch-1 sp, ch 1, hdc in next ch-1 sp, ★ ch 2, skip next ch-2 sp, (work Puff St, ch 2) twice in next ch-2 sp, skip next ch-2 sp, hdc in next ch-1 sp, ch 1, (sc, ch 2, sc) in next ch-1 sp, ch 1, hdc in next ch-1 sp; repeat from ★ across to last 2 dc, skip next dc, dc in last dc; do **not** finish off: 75 sps.

EDGING

Rnd 1: Do **not** turn; working in end of rows, work (beginning Puff St, ch 2, Puff St) in first row, ch 2, † skip next row, 8 dc in next row, ch 2, [skip next row, (work Puff St, ch 2) twice in next row, skip next row, 8 dc in next row, ch 2] across to last 2 rows, skip next row, (work Puff St, ch 2) 4 times in last row †; skip next sp, 8 dc in free loops of next ch *(Fig. 26b, page 142)* (at base of next 4-dc group), ch 2, ★ skip next 2 sps, (work Puff St in free loops of ch at base of next Puff St, ch 2) twice, skip next 2 sps, 8 dc in free loops of next ch (at base of next 4-dc group), ch 2; repeat from ★ across to last 2 sps, skip next sp, (work Puff St, ch 2) 4 times in last sp; working in end of rows, repeat from † to † once; working in sps across Row 105, skip first ch-1 sp, 8 dc in next ch-2 sp, ch 2, [skip next 2 sps, (work Puff St, ch 2) twice in next ch-2 sp, skip next 2 sps, 8 dc in next ch-2 sp, ch 2] across to last ch-1 sp, skip last ch-1 sp, (work Puff St, ch 2) twice in same sp as beginning Puff St; join with slip st to top of beginning Puff St: 164 Puff Sts and 624 dc.

Rnd 2: Slip st in first ch-2 sp, work (beginning Puff St, ch 2, Puff St) in same sp, ★ † ch 3, skip next dc, dc in next 6 dc, ch 3, [skip next ch-2 sp, work (Puff St, ch 2, Puff St) in next ch-2 sp, ch 3, skip next dc, dc in next 6 dc, ch 3] across to within one ch-2 sp of corner 4-Puff St group, skip next ch-2 sp, (work Puff St, ch 2) twice in next ch-2 sp, skip next corner ch-2 sp †, work (Puff St, ch 2, Puff St) in next ch-2 sp; repeat from ★ 2 times **more**, then repeat from † to † once; join with slip st to top of beginning Puff St, do **not** finish off.

Continued on page 104.

GRANDEUR Continued from page 102.

Rnd 3: Slip st in first ch-2 sp, work (beginning Puff St, ch 2, Puff St, ch 1, Puff St, ch 2, Puff St) in same sp, ★ † [ch 1, skip next dc, dc in next 4 dc, ch 1, skip next ch-3 sp, work (Puff St, ch 2, Puff St, ch 1, Puff St, ch 2, Puff St) in next ch-2 sp] across to next corner ch-2 sp, ch 2, skip corner ch-2 sp †, work (Puff St, ch 2, Puff St, ch 1, Puff St, ch 2, Puff St) in next ch-2 sp; repeat from ★ 2 times **more**, then repeat from † to † once; join with slip st to top of beginning Puff St.

Rnd 4: Slip st in first ch-2 sp, work (beginning Puff St, ch 2, Puff St) in same sp, ★ † ch 1, work Puff St in next ch-1 sp, ch 1, work (Puff St, ch 2, Puff St) in next ch-2 sp, ch 1, [skip next dc, dc in next 2 dc, ch 1, skip next ch-1 sp, work (Puff St, ch 2, Puff St) in next ch-2 sp, ch 1, work Puff St in next ch-1 sp, ch 1, work (Puff St, ch 2, Puff St) in next ch-2 sp, ch 1] across to next corner ch-2 sp, skip corner ch-2 sp †, work (Puff St, ch 2, Puff St) in next ch-2 sp; repeat from ★ 2 times **more**, then repeat from † to † once; join with slip st to top of beginning Puff St.

Rnd 5: Slip st in first ch-2 sp, work (beginning Puff St, ch 2, Puff St) in same sp, ch 1, [work (Puff St, ch 2, Puff St) in next sp, ch 1] 3 times, ★ † sc in next 2 dc, ch 1, skip next ch-1 sp, [work (Puff St, ch 2, Puff St) in next sp, ch 1] 4 times †, repeat from † to † across to next corner ch-1 sp, skip corner ch-1 sp, [work (Puff St, ch 2, Puff St) in next sp, ch 1] 4 times; repeat from ★ 2 times **more**, then repeat from † to † across to last corner ch-1 sp, skip last corner ch-1 sp; join with slip st to top of beginning Puff St.

Rnd 6: Slip st in first ch-2 sp, ch 6, slip st in fourth ch from hook, ★ † (ch 1, dc in next sp, work Picot) 6 times, ch 2, [skip next sc, sc in next sc, ch 2, skip next ch-1 sp, dc in next sp, work Picot, (ch 1, dc in next sp, work Picot) 6 times, ch 2] across to next corner ch-1 sp, skip corner ch-1 sp †, dc in next sp, work Picot; repeat from ★ 2 times **more**, then repeat from † to † once; join with slip st to third ch of beginning ch-6, finish off.

COUNTRY PLEASURES Continued from page 98.

Row 9: Ch 2, turn; dc in next 5 dc, † working in **front** of next dc, work FP Cluster, skip dc behind FP Cluster, dc in next 2 dc, working in **front** of last dc worked into, work FP Cluster, dc in same st as last dc and in next dc, working in **front** of next dc, work FP Cluster, skip dc behind FP Cluster †, ★ dc in next 6 dc, skip next 2 dc, dc in next 6 dc, repeat from † to † once; repeat from ★ across to last 6 dc, dc in next 4 dc, decrease.

Row 10: Ch 2, turn; dc in next 7 sts, 3 dc in next FP Cluster, ★ dc in next 8 sts, skip next 2 dc, dc in next 8 sts, 3 dc in next FP Cluster; repeat from ★ across to last 8 sts, dc in next 6 sts, decrease changing to Ecru.

Repeat Rows 3-10, until Afghan measures approximately 66" from beginning ch at point, ending by working Row 9.

Last Row: Ch 2, turn; dc in next 7 sts, 3 dc in next FP Cluster, ★ dc in next 8 sts, skip next 2 dc, dc in next 8 sts, 3 dc in next FP Cluster; repeat from ★ across to last 8 sts, dc in next 6 sts, decrease; finish off.

Holding 10 strands of Green together, add fringe at each point across short edges of Afghan *(Figs. 31a & c, page 143)*.

Rnd 5: Ch 3, dc in next 2 sc, work FPdc around next FPdc, (dc in next 3 sc, work FPdc around next FPdc) 53 times, † dc in next 4 sc, ★ 2 dc in next sc, work FPdc around next FPdc, 2 dc in next sc, dc in next 4 sc; repeat from ★ 2 times **more**, work FPdc around next FPdc †, (dc in next 3 sc, work FPdc around next FPdc) 54 times, repeat from † to † once; join with slip st to first dc: 380 dc and 116 FPdc.

Rnd 6: Ch 1, sc in same st and in next 2 dc, work FPsc around next FPdc, (sc in next 3 dc, work FPsc around next FPdc) 53 times, † sc in next 5 dc, 2 sc in next dc, work FPsc around next FPdc, place marker around FPsc just made for joining placement, (2 sc in next dc, sc in next 3 dc) twice, work FPsc around next FPdc, (sc in next 3 dc, 2 sc in next dc) twice, work FPsc around next FPdc, place marker around FPsc just made for joining placement, 2 sc in next dc, sc in next 5 dc, work FPsc around next FPdc †, (sc in next 3 dc, work FPsc around next FPdc) 54 times, repeat from † to † once; join with slip st to first sc, finish off: 392 sc and 116 FPsc.

ASSEMBLY

Place two Strips with **wrong** sides together and bottom edges at same end. With Rust and working through inside loops only, whipstitch Strips together *(Fig. 30a, page 143)*, beginning in first marked FPsc and ending in next marked FPsc. Do **not** remove markers on outside edge of first Strip.

EDGING

With **right** side facing, working across short end and in Back Loops Only *(Fig. 25, page 142)*, join Rust with slip st in marked FPsc at top of first Strip, remove all markers; ch 1, sc in same st and in each sc across to within one sc of next joining, † decrease, (sc in next 19 sts, decrease) 9 times †, sc in each sc across to within one sc of next joining, repeat from † to † once, sc in each sc around; join with slip st to first sc, finish off.

BRICKS OF COLOR

The colorful "bricks" in this striking throw are "built" using only basic stitches. The pattern is perfect for using up scraps of yarn. Black rows separate our seven shades, and long double crochet stitches form the vertical lines.

Finished Size: 49" x 61"

MATERIALS
Worsted Weight Yarn:
Black - 10 ounces,
(280 grams, 565 yards)
Scraps - 48 ounces,
(1,360 grams, 2,715 yards) **total**
Note: Each 3 row repeat requires
56 1/2 yards of scrap yarn.
Crochet hook, size I (5.50 mm) **or** size needed for gauge

GAUGE: In pattern, 13 sts = 4 1/4";
Rows 1-13 = 4"

Gauge Swatch: 4 1/2"w x 4"h
Ch 15 **loosely**.
Work same as Afghan for 13 rows.
Finish off.

STITCH GUIDE

LONG DOUBLE CROCHET *(abbreviated LDC)*
YO, insert hook in st 3 rows **below** next sc, YO and pull up a loop even with last sc made, (YO and draw through 2 loops on hook) twice *(Fig. 22, page 141)*. Skip sc behind LDC.

AFGHAN BODY

With Black, ch 150 **loosely**.
Row 1 (Right side)**:** Sc in second ch from hook and in each ch across changing to scrap color desired in last sc *(Fig. 27a, page 142)*: 149 sc.
Row 2: Ch 1, turn; sc in each sc across.
Row 3: Ch 3 **(counts as first dc, now and throughout)**, turn; dc in next sc and in each sc across.
Row 4: Ch 1, turn; sc in each dc across changing to Black in last sc.
Row 5: Ch 1, turn; sc in first 4 sc, (work LDC, sc in next 4 sc) across changing to scrap color desired in last sc.
Row 6: Ch 1, turn; sc in each st across.
Row 7: Ch 3, turn; dc in next sc and in each sc across.
Row 8: Ch 1, turn; sc in each dc across changing to Black in last sc.
Repeat Rows 5-8 until Afghan measures approximately 60" from beginning ch, ending by working Row 5, do **not** change colors, do **not** finish off.

EDGING

Rnd 1: Ch 1, do **not** turn; sc evenly around entire Afghan working 3 sc in each corner; join with slip st to first sc.
Rnd 2: Ch 1, sc in each sc around working 3 sc in center sc of each corner 3-sc group; join with slip st to first sc, finish off.

REGAL TONES

The richly toned panels in this regal wrap get their opulent look from front post double crochet clusters. An openwork edging offers a splendid finish for the afghan, which is crocheted holding two strands of yarn together and using a jumbo hook.

Finished Size: 48" x 63"

MATERIALS

Worsted Weight Yarn:
  Lt Brown - 12 ounces, (340 grams, 890 yards)
  Brown - 7 ounces, (200 grams, 520 yards)
  Gold - 7 ounces, (200 grams, 520 yards)
  Rust - 7 ounces, (200 grams, 520 yards)
  Green - 7 ounces, (200 grams, 520 yards)
Crochet hook, size Q (15.00 mm)
Yarn needle

Note: Entire Afghan is worked holding two strands of yarn together.

GAUGE: Each Center = 7½" wide;
        11 rows = 7"

STITCH GUIDE

FRONT POST DOUBLE CROCHET
(abbreviated FPdc)
YO, insert hook from **front** to **back** around post of st indicated, YO and pull up a loop *(Fig. 11, page 139)*, (YO and draw through 2 loops on hook) twice. Skip sc behind FPdc.

FRONT POST DOUBLE CROCHET CLUSTER
(abbreviated FPdc Cluster)
★ YO, insert hook from **front** to **back** around post of dc indicated *(Fig. 9, page 139)*, YO and pull up a loop even with last st, YO and draw through 2 loops on hook; repeat from ★ 2 times **more**, YO and draw through all 4 loops on hook *(Fig. 15a, page 140)*. Skip sc behind FPdc Cluster.

PANEL (Make 4)
CENTER

Note: Make one Center in each of the following colors: Brown, Gold, Rust, and Green.
Ch 12 **loosely**.

Row 1: Sc in second ch from hook and in each ch across: 11 sc.

Row 2 (Right side)**:** Ch 3 **(counts as first dc, now and throughout)**, turn; dc in next sc and in each sc across.
Note: Loop a short piece of yarn around any stitch to mark Row 2 as **right** side and bottom edge.
Row 3: Ch 1, turn; sc in each dc across.
Row 4: Ch 3, turn; work FPdc around st one row **below** next sc, (dc in next 3 sc, work FPdc around st one row **below** next sc) twice, dc in last sc.
Row 5: Ch 1, turn; sc in each st across.
Row 6: Ch 3, turn; work FPdc around first FPdc one row **below** next sc, dc in next sc, skip next sc, work FPdc Cluster around dc one row **below** next sc, dc in next sc, work FPdc around next FPdc one row **below** next sc, dc in next sc, work FPdc Cluster around dc one row **below** sc just worked into, dc in next sc, work FPdc around next FPdc one row **below** next sc, dc in last sc.
Rows 7-9: Repeat Rows 5 and 6 once, then repeat Row 5 once **more**.
Row 10: Ch 3, turn; work FPdc around first FPdc one row **below** next sc, dc in next 2 sc, work FPdc Cluster around dc one row **below** next sc, dc in next sc, work FPdc Cluster around dc one row **below** next sc, dc in next 2 sc, work FPdc around next FPdc one row **below** next sc, dc in last sc.
Row 11: Ch 1, turn; sc in each st across.
Row 12: Ch 3, turn; work FPdc around first FPdc one row **below** next sc, dc in next 3 sc, work FPdc Cluster around dc one row **below** next sc, dc in next 3 sc, work FPdc around next FPdc one row **below** next sc, dc in last sc.
Row 13: Ch 1, turn; sc in each st across.
Row 14: Ch 3, turn; work FPdc around first FPdc one row **below** next sc, dc in next 7 sc, work FPdc around next FPdc one row **below** next sc, dc in last sc.
Row 15: Ch 1, turn; sc in each st across.
Rows 16-87: Repeat Rows 4-15, 6 times.
Do **not** finish off.

Continued on page 115.

BRILLIANT RIPPLES

*Ablaze with color, this throw captures the brilliance of autumn.
We used scrap yarns enhanced with black to fashion the ripples
of "leaves," which are created using long double crochets.*

Finished Size: 46" x 60"

MATERIALS

Worsted Weight Yarn:
   Black - 22 ounces, (620 grams, 1,245 yards)
   Scraps - 37 ounces,
      (1,050 grams, 2,095 yards) **total**
   Note: Each scrap row requires 35 yards.
   Crochet hook, size I (5.50 mm) **or** size needed
      for gauge

GAUGE: Each repeat from point to point = 3¹/₂";
      6 rows = 4"

Gauge Swatch: 7"w x 4"h
Ch 41 **loosely**.
Work same as Afghan for 6 rows.
Do **not** change colors, finish off.

STITCH GUIDE

> **LONG DOUBLE CROCHET (abbreviated LDC)**
> YO, working **around** next ch-2, insert hook in st or sp
> indicated one row **below** ch-2, YO and pull up a loop even
> with last st made, (YO and draw through 2 loops on hook)
> twice *(Fig. 22, page 141)*.

AFGHAN BODY

With Black, ch 261 **loosely**.

Row 1 (Right side)**:** Dc in fourth ch from hook **(3 skipped
chs count as first dc)**, ch 2, skip next 3 chs, 2 dc in next ch,
ch 2, skip next 3 chs, (2 dc, ch 3, 2 dc) in next ch, ★ (ch 2,
skip next 3 chs, 2 dc in next ch) twice, skip next 3 chs, (2 dc in
next ch, ch 2, skip next 3 chs) twice, (2 dc, ch 3, 2 dc) in next
ch; repeat from ★ across to last 9 chs, ch 2, skip next 3 chs,
2 dc in next ch, ch 2, skip next 3 chs, dc in last 2 chs changing
to Scrap color desired in last dc *(Fig. 27a, page 142)*:
156 dc and 65 sps.
Note: Loop a short piece of yarn around any stitch to mark
Row 1 as **right** side.

Row 2: Ch 3 **(counts as first dc, now and throughout)**,
turn; skip next dc, work LDC in center ch of first 3 skipped chs
of beginning ch, ch 2, skip next 2 dc, work 2 LDC in center ch
of next 3 skipped chs of beginning ch, ch 2, skip next 2 dc,
(2 dc, ch 3, 2 dc) in next ch-3 sp, ★ (ch 2, skip next 2 dc,
work 2 LDC in center ch of next 3 skipped chs of beginning ch)
twice, skip next 4 dc, (work 2 LDC in center ch of next
3 skipped chs of beginning ch, ch 2, skip next 2 dc) twice,
(2 dc, ch 3, 2 dc) in next ch-3 sp; repeat from ★ across to last
6 dc, ch 2, skip next 2 dc, work 2 LDC in center ch of next
3 skipped chs of beginning ch, ch 2, skip next 2 dc, work LDC
in center ch of last 3 skipped chs of beginning ch, skip next dc,
dc in last dc: 102 LDC and 54 dc.

Row 3: Ch 3, turn; skip next LDC, work 2 LDC in sp **between**
next 2 dc (one row **below**) *(Fig. 28, page 142)*, ch 2, skip
next 2 LDC, work 2 LDC in sp **between** next 2 dc, ch 2, skip
next 2 dc, (2 dc, ch 3, 2 dc) in next ch-3 sp, ch 2, skip next
2 dc, work 2 LDC in sp **between** next 2 dc, ch 2, skip next
2 LDC, work 2 LDC in sp **between** next 2 dc, ★ skip next
4 LDC, work 2 LDC in sp **between** next 2 dc, ch 2, skip next
2 LDC, work 2 LDC in sp **between** next 2 dc, ch 2, skip next
2 dc, (2 dc, ch 3, 2 dc) in next ch-3 sp, ch 2, skip next 2 dc,
work 2 LDC in sp **between** next 2 dc, ch 2, skip next 2 LDC,
work 2 LDC in sp **between** next 2 dc; repeat from ★ across to
last 2 sts, skip next LDC, dc in last dc changing to Black.

Row 4: Ch 3, turn; skip next 2 LDC, work 2 LDC in sp **between**
next 2 LDC (one row **below**), ch 2, skip next 2 LDC, work
2 LDC in sp **between** next 2 dc, ch 2, skip next 2 dc, (2 dc,
ch 3, 2 dc) in next ch-3 sp, ch 2, skip next 2 dc, work 2 LDC in
sp **between** next 2 dc, ch 2, skip next 2 LDC, work 2 LDC in sp
between next 2 LDC, ★ skip next 4 LDC, work 2 LDC in sp
between next 2 LDC, ch 2, skip next 2 LDC, work 2 LDC in sp
between next 2 dc, ch 2, skip next 2 dc, (2 dc, ch 3, 2 dc) in
next ch-3 sp, ch 2, skip next 2 dc, work 2 LDC in sp **between**
next 2 dc, ch 2, skip next 2 LDC, work 2 LDC in sp **between**
next 2 LDC; repeat from ★ across to last 3 sts, skip next 2 LDC,
dc in last dc changing to scrap color desired.

Continued on page 115.

SIGNS OF FALL

This afghan portrays one of our favorite signs of fall — those spectacular rust and gold leaves. The leaf motifs take shape from specially placed squares, and simple slip stitches form the stems.

Finished Size: 54" x 66"

MATERIALS

Worsted Weight Yarn:

Cream - 35 ounces, (990 grams, 2,400 yards)

Lt Brown - 7 ounces, (200 grams, 480 yards)

Brown - 3 ounces, (90 grams, 205 yards)

Yellow - 3 ounces, (90 grams, 205 yards)

Gold - 3 ounces, (90 grams, 205 yards)

Rust - 3 ounces, (90 grams, 205 yards)

Crochet hook, size I (5.50 mm) **or** size needed for gauge

Yarn needle

GAUGE SWATCH: Each Square = 3"
Work same as Square A.

Referring to the Key, page 114, make the number of Squares specified in the colors indicated.

SQUARE A

With color indicated, ch 4; join with slip st to form a ring.

Rnd 1 (Right side)**:** Ch 3 **(counts as first dc, now and throughout)**, 2 dc in ring, ch 2, (3 dc in ring, ch 2) 3 times; join with slip st to first dc: 12 dc and 4 ch-2 sps.
Note: Loop a short piece of yarn around any stitch to mark Rnd 1 as **right** side.
Rnd 2: Slip st in next 2 dc and in next ch-2 sp, ch 3, (2 dc, ch 2, 3 dc) in same sp, ch 1, ★ (3 dc, ch 2, 3 dc) in next ch-2 sp, ch 1; repeat from ★ 2 times **more**; join with slip st to first dc, finish off: 24 dc and 8 sps.

SQUARE B

With Cream, ch 4; join with slip st to form a ring.

Rnd 1 (Right side)**:** Ch 5 **(counts as first dc plus ch 2)**, 3 dc in ring, cut Cream, with second color indicated, YO and draw through, ch 1, (3 dc, ch 2, 3 dc) in ring, cut second color, with Cream, YO and draw through, ch 1, 2 dc in ring; join with slip st to first dc: 12 dc and 4 ch-2 sps.
Note: Mark Rnd 1 as **right** side.
Rnd 2: Slip st in first ch-2 sp, ch 3, (2 dc, ch 2, 3 dc) in same sp, ch 1, 3 dc in next ch-2 sp, cut Cream, with second color, YO and draw through, ch 1, 3 dc in same sp, ch 1, (3 dc, ch 2, 3 dc) in next ch-2 sp, ch 1, 3 dc in next ch-2 sp, cut second color, with Cream, YO and draw through, ch 1, 3 dc in same sp, ch 1; join with slip st to first dc, finish off: 24 dc and 8 sps.

ASSEMBLY

With matching color, using Placement Diagram as a guide, page 114, and working through inside loops only, whipstitch Squares together **(Fig. 30a, page 143)**, forming 17 vertical strips of 21 Squares each, beginning in second ch of first corner ch-2, and ending in first ch of next corner ch-2; whipstitch strips together in same manner.

STEMS

Note: Keep working yarn on wrong side of Afghan.

With **right** side facing and Lt Brown, insert hook in corner of Square as indicated on Placement Diagram and pull up a loop, working diagonally, ★ insert hook in Square, YO and draw through **loosely** through loop on hook; repeat from ★ evenly spaced across to next corner; finish off.
Repeat for each Stem.

Continued on page 114.

EDGING

Rnd 1: With **right** side facing, join Cream with sc in any corner ch-2 sp *(see Joining With Sc, page 142)*; ch 2, sc in same sp, sc in each dc and in each sp and joining across to next corner ch-2 sp, ★ (sc, ch 2, sc) in corner ch-2 sp, sc in each dc and in each sp and joining across to next corner ch-2 sp; repeat from ★ 2 times **more**; join with slip st to first sc, finish off: 756 sc and 4 ch-2 sps.

Rnd 2: With **right** side facing, join Lt Brown with sc in any corner ch-2 sp; ch 2, sc in same sp, sc in each sc across to next corner ch-2 sp, ★ (sc, ch 2, sc) in corner ch-2 sp, sc in each sc across to next corner ch-2 sp; repeat from ★ 2 times **more**; join with slip st to first sc: 764 sc and 4 ch-2 sps.

Rnd 3: Slip st in first ch-2 sp, ch 5 **(counts as first hdc plus ch 3, now and throughout)**, hdc in same sp, ch 1, skip next sc, (hdc in next sc, ch 1, skip next sc) across to next corner ch-2 sp, ★ (hdc, ch 3, hdc) in corner ch-2 sp, ch 1, skip next sc, (hdc in next sc, ch 1, skip next sc) across to next corner ch-2 sp; repeat from ★ 2 times **more**; join with slip st to first hdc, finish off: 388 hdc and 388 sps.

Rnd 4: With **right** side facing, join Cream with sc in any corner ch-3 sp; ch 3, sc in same sp, ch 1, (sc in next ch-1 sp, ch 1) across to next corner ch-3 sp, ★ (sc, ch 3, sc) in corner ch-3 sp, ch 1, (sc in next ch-1 sp, ch 1) across to next corner ch-3 sp; repeat from ★ 2 times **more**; join with slip st to first sc, finish off: 392 hdc and 392 sps.

Rnd 5: With **right** side facing, join Lt Brown with slip st in any corner ch-3 sp; ch 5, hdc in same sp, ch 1, ★ (hdc in next ch-1 sp, ch 1) across to next corner ch-3 sp, (hdc, ch 3, hdc) in corner ch-3 sp, ch 1; repeat from ★ 2 times **more**, (hdc in next ch-1 sp, ch 1) across; join with slip st to first hdc: 396 hdc and 396 sps.

Rnd 6: Slip st in next ch-3 sp, ch 1, sc in same sp, ch 3, (sc in next sp, ch 3) around; join with slip st to first sc, finish off.

KEY

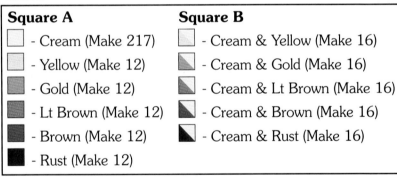

Square A
- Cream (Make 217)
- Yellow (Make 12)
- Gold (Make 12)
- Lt Brown (Make 12)
- Brown (Make 12)
- Rust (Make 12)

Square B
- Cream & Yellow (Make 16)
- Cream & Gold (Make 16)
- Cream & Lt Brown (Make 16)
- Cream & Brown (Make 16)
- Cream & Rust (Make 16)

PLACEMENT DIAGRAM

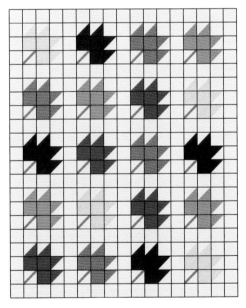

BRILLIANT RIPPLES Continued from page 110.

Row 5: Ch 3, turn; skip next 2 LDC, work 2 LDC in sp **between** next 2 LDC (one row **below**), ch 2, skip next 2 LDC, work 2 LDC in sp **between** next 2 dc, ch 2, skip next 2 dc, (2 dc, ch 3, 2 dc) in next ch-3 sp, ch 2, skip next 2 dc, work 2 LDC in sp **between** next 2 dc, ch 2, skip next 2 LDC, work 2 LDC in sp **between** next 2 LDC, ★ skip next 4 LDC, work 2 LDC in sp **between** next 2 LDC, ch 2, skip next 2 LDC, work 2 LDC in sp **between** next 2 dc, ch 2, skip next 2 dc, (2 dc, ch 3, 2 dc) in next ch-3 sp, ch 2, skip next 2 dc, work 2 LDC in sp **between** next 2 dc, ch 2, skip next 2 LDC, work 2 LDC in sp **between** next 2 LDC; repeat from ★ across to last 3 sts, skip next 2 LDC, dc in last dc.

Row 6: Ch 3, turn; skip next 2 LDC, work 2 LDC in sp **between** next 2 LDC (one row **below**), ch 2, skip next 2 LDC, work 2 LDC in sp **between** next 2 dc, ch 2, skip next 2 dc, (2 dc, ch 3, 2 dc) in next ch-3 sp, ch 2, skip next 2 dc, work 2 LDC in sp **between** next 2 LDC, ★ skip next 4 LDC, work 2 LDC in sp **between** next 2 LDC, ch 2, skip next 2 LDC, work 2 LDC in sp **between** next 2 dc, ch 2, skip next 2 dc, (2 dc, ch 3, 2 dc) in next ch-3 sp, ch 2, skip next 2 dc, work 2 LDC in sp **between** next 2 dc, ch 2, skip next 2 LDC, work 2 LDC in sp **between** next 2 LDC; repeat from ★ across to last 3 sts, skip next 2 LDC, dc in last dc changing to Black.

Repeat Rows 4-6 until Afghan measures approximately 59" from beginning ch at point, ending by working Row 6.

Last Row: Ch 3, turn; skip next 2 LDC, work 2 LDC in sp **between** next 2 LDC (one row **below**), sc in next 2 LDC, work 2 LDC in sp **between** next 2 dc, sc in next 2 dc, (sc, ch 3, sc) in next ch-3 sp, sc in next 2 dc, work 2 LDC in sp **between** next 2 dc, sc in next 2 LDC, work 2 LDC in sp **between** next 2 LDC, ★ skip next 4 LDC, work 2 LDC in sp **between** next 2 LDC, sc in next 2 LDC, work 2 LDC in sp **between** next 2 dc, sc in next 2 dc, (sc, ch 3, sc) in next ch-3 sp, sc in next 2 dc, work 2 LDC in sp **between** next 2 dc, sc in next 2 LDC, work 2 LDC in sp **between** next 2 LDC; repeat from ★ across to last 3 sts, skip next 2 LDC, dc in last dc; finish off.

Holding 12 strands of Black together, add fringe at each point across short edges of Afghan *(Figs. 31a & c, page 143)*.

REGAL TONES Continued from page 108.

EDGING

Rnd 1: Ch 1, turn; 3 sc in first sc, sc in next 9 sc, 3 sc in last sc, ch 1; working in end of rows, skip first row, (sc in next row, ch 1, skip next row) across; working in free loops of beginning ch *(Fig. 26b, page 142)*, 3 sc in ch at base of first sc, sc in next 9 chs, 3 sc in last ch, ch 1; working in end of rows, skip first row, (sc in next row, ch 1, skip next row) across; join with slip st to first sc, finish off.

Rnd 2: With **right** side facing, join Lt Brown with slip st in center sc of top right corner 3-sc group; ch 4 **(counts as first dc plus ch 1, now and throughout)**, (dc, ch 1) twice in same st, † skip next sc, (dc in next sc, ch 1, skip next sc) 5 times, (dc, ch 1) 3 times in next sc, (dc in next ch-1 sp, ch 1) across to next corner 3-sc group, skip next sc †, (dc, ch 1) 3 times in center sc, repeat from † to † once; join with slip st to first dc.

Rnd 3: Ch 1, sc in same st and in each ch-1 sp and each dc around; join with slip st to first sc, finish off.

ASSEMBLY

Afghan is assembled by joining Panels, with bottom edges at the same end and working from left to right, in the following color sequence: Gold, Rust, Green, Brown.

Using Lt Brown and working through both loops, whipstitch Panels together *(Fig. 30b, page 143)*, beginning in first corner sc and ending in next corner sc.

BORDER

Rnd 1: With **right** side facing, join Lt Brown with slip st in corner sc at top right; ch 4, (dc, ch 1) twice in same st, † skip next sc, (dc in next sc, ch 1, skip next sc) 7 times, ★ (dc in next joining sc, ch 1) twice, skip next sc, (dc in next sc, skip next sc, ch 1) 7 times; repeat from ★ across to next corner sc, (dc, ch 1) 3 times in corner sc, skip next sc, (dc in next sc, ch 1, skip next sc) across to next corner sc †, (dc, ch 1) 3 times in corner sc; repeat from † to † once; join with slip st to first dc.

Rnd 2: Ch 1, sc in same st and in each dc and each ch-1 sp around; join with slip st to first sc, finish off.

SPIDERWEB

The intricate pattern of this throw reminds us of beautifully spun spiderwebs. Strands of taupe and natural yarns are held together as you crochet to create the homespun hue.

Finished Size: 46" x 68"

MATERIALS

Worsted Weight Yarn:
Taupe - 24 ounces,
(680 grams, 1,580 yards)
Natural - 24 ounces,
(680 grams, 1,580 yards)
Crochet hook, size N (9.00 mm) **or** size needed for gauge

Note: Entire Afghan is worked holding one strand Taupe and one strand Natural together.

GAUGE: 7 dc = 3"; 11 rows = 8"

Gauge Swatch: 3¼"w x 5"h
Ch 25 **loosely**.
Work same as Afghan for 8 rows.
Finish off.

STITCH GUIDE

REVERSE HALF DOUBLE CROCHET
 (abbreviated reverse hdc)
Working from **left** to **right**, YO, insert hook in sc indicated to right of hook, YO and draw through, under, and to left of loops on hook (3 loops on hook), YO and draw through all 3 loops on hook (**reverse hdc made, *Figs. 24a-d, page 141)*.

AFGHAN BODY

Ch 105 **loosely**.

Row 1: Dc in fourth ch from hook and in each ch across: 103 sts.

Row 2: Ch 3 **(counts as first dc, now and throughout)**, turn; dc in next 2 dc, ch 1, skip next dc, ★ dc in next 15 dc, ch 1, skip next dc; repeat from ★ across to last 3 sts, dc in last 3 sts.

Row 3: Ch 3, turn; dc in next 2 dc, ch 1, ★ dc in next dc, ch 1, (skip next dc, dc in next dc, ch 1) 7 times; repeat from ★ across to last 3 dc, dc in last 3 dc.

Row 4: Ch 3, turn; dc in next 2 dc, ch 1, ★ dc in next dc, (dc in next ch-1 sp and in next dc) 7 times, ch 1; repeat from ★ across to last 3 dc, dc in last 3 dc.

Row 5: Ch 3, turn; dc in next 2 dc, ch 1, ★ dc in next 15 dc, ch 1; repeat from ★ across to last 3 dc, dc in last 3 dc.

Row 6: Ch 3, turn; dc in next 2 dc, ch 1, dc in next 3 dc, ★ ch 3, (skip next dc, tr in next dc) 4 times, ch 3, skip next dc, dc in next 3 dc, ch 1, dc in next 3 dc; repeat from ★ across.

Row 7: Ch 3, turn; dc in next 2 dc, ch 1, dc in next 3 dc, ★ ch 3, sc in next 4 tr, ch 3, dc in next 3 dc, ch 1, dc in next 3 dc; repeat from ★ across.

Rows 8-10: Ch 3, turn; dc in next 2 dc, ch 1, dc in next 3 dc, ★ ch 3, sc in next 4 sc, ch 3, dc in next 3 dc, ch 1, dc in next 3 dc; repeat from ★ across.

Row 11: Ch 3, turn; dc in next 2 dc, ch 1, dc in next 3 dc, ★ (ch 1, tr in next sc) 4 times, (ch 1, dc in next 3 dc) twice; repeat from ★ across.

Row 12: Ch 3, turn; dc in next 2 dc, ch 1, dc in next 3 dc, ★ (dc in next ch-1 sp and in next tr) 4 times, dc in next ch-1 sp and in next 3 dc, ch 1, dc in next 3 dc; repeat from ★ across.

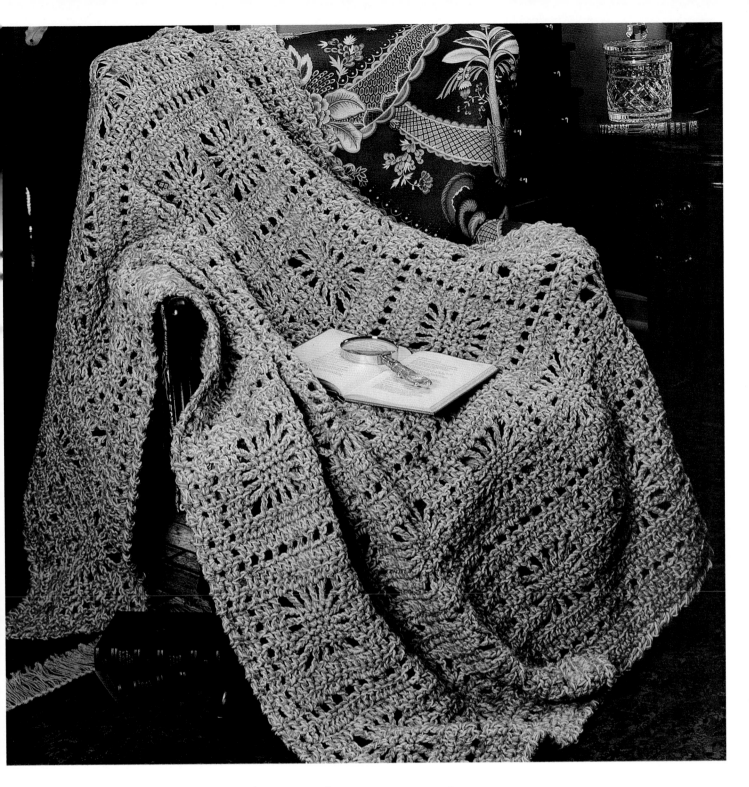

Row 13: Ch 3, turn; dc in next 2 dc, ch 1, ★ dc in next 15 dc, ch 1; repeat from ★ across to last 3 dc, dc in last 3 dc. Repeat Rows 3-13 until Afghan measures approximately 67" from beginning ch, ending by working Row 4.

Last Row: Ch 3, turn; dc in next dc and in each dc and each ch-1 sp across; do **not** finish off: 103 dc.

EDGING

Rnd 1 (Right side)**:** Ch 1, turn; 3 sc in first dc, sc in each dc across to last dc, 3 sc in last dc; work 154 sc evenly spaced across end of rows; working in free loops of beginning ch **(Fig. 26b, page 142)**, 3 sc in first ch, sc in each ch across to last ch, 3 sc in last ch; work 154 sc evenly spaced across end of rows; join with slip st to first sc: 522 sc.

Rnd 2: Ch 2, working from **left** to **right**, skip next sc, ★ work reverse hdc in next sc, ch 1, skip next sc; repeat from ★ around; join with slip st to base of beginning ch-2, finish off.

117

AUTUMN SPLENDOR

Imagine wrapping yourself in the splendor of autumn! It's easy when you make this rippled throw in rich rust accented with deep green. Variegated yarn adds a sprinkling of color.

Finished Size: 44" x 58"

MATERIALS
Worsted Weight Yarn:
　　Rust - 32 ounces, (910 grams, 2,195 yards)
　　Green - 10 ounces, (280 grams, 685 yards)
　　Variegated - 9 ounces, (260 grams, 615 yards)
Crochet hook, size J (6.00 mm) **or** size needed
　　for gauge

Note: Entire Afghan is worked holding two strands of yarn
　　together.

GAUGE: Each repeat from point to point = 7¼";
　　　　7 rows = 6"

Gauge Swatch: 14½"w x 6"h
Ch 42 **loosely**.
Work same as Afghan for 7 rows.
Finish off.

STITCH GUIDE

> **DECREASE**
> ★ YO, insert hook in **next** st or sp, YO and pull up a loop, YO and draw through 2 loops on hook; repeat from ★ once **more**, YO and draw through all 3 loops on hook **(counts as one dc)**.

Holding 2 strands of Rust together, ch 122 **loosely**.
Row 1 (Right side)**:** 2 Dc in third ch from hook **(2 skipped chs count as first dc)**, ★ † dc in next 6 chs, decrease, skip next 2 chs, decrease, dc in next 6 chs †, (dc, ch 1, dc) in next 2 chs; repeat from ★ 4 times **more**, then repeat from † to † once, 3 dc in last ch: 110 dc and 10 ch-1 sps.
Note: Loop a short piece of yarn around any stitch to mark Row 1 as **right** side.
Row 2: Ch 3 **(counts as first dc, now and throughout)**, turn; 2 dc in same st, dc in next 6 dc, decrease, skip next 2 dc, decrease, ★ dc in next 5 dc and in next ch-1 sp, (dc, ch 1, dc) in next 2 dc, dc in next ch-1 sp and in next 5 dc, decrease, skip next 2 dc, decrease; repeat from ★ 4 times **more**, dc in next 6 dc, 3 dc in last dc; finish off.

Row 3: With **right** side facing and holding 2 strands of Green together, join yarn with sc in first dc *(see Joining With Sc, page 142)*; ch 1, skip next dc, (sc in next dc, ch 1, skip next dc) 3 times, sc in next 4 dc, ★ ch 1, (skip next dc, sc in next dc, ch 1) 3 times, sc in next 2 dc, ch 1, (sc in next dc, ch 1, skip next dc) 3 times, sc in next 4 dc; repeat from ★ 4 times **more**, (ch 1, skip next dc, sc in next dc) 4 times; finish off: 72 sc and 48 ch-1 sps.
Row 4: With **wrong** side facing and holding one strand of Rust and one strand of Variegated together, join yarn with slip st in first sc; ch 3, 2 dc in same st, ★ † (dc in next ch-1 sp and in next sc) 3 times, decrease, skip next 2 sc, decrease, (dc in next sc and in next ch-1 sp) 3 times †, (dc, ch 1, dc) in next 2 sc; repeat from ★ 4 times **more**, then repeat from † to † once, 3 dc in last sc: 110 dc and 10 ch-1 sps.
Row 5: Ch 3, turn; 2 dc in same st, dc in next 6 dc, decrease, skip next 2 dc, decrease, ★ dc in next 5 dc and in next ch-1 sp, (dc, ch 1, dc) in next 2 dc, dc in next ch-1 sp and in next 5 dc, decrease, skip next 2 dc, decrease; repeat from ★ 4 times **more**, dc in next 6 dc, 3 dc in last dc; finish off.
Row 6: With **wrong** side facing and holding 2 strands of Green together, join yarn with sc in first dc; ch 1, skip next dc, (sc in next dc, ch 1, skip next dc) 3 times, sc in next 4 dc, ★ ch 1, (skip next dc, sc in next dc, ch 1) 3 times, sc in next 2 dc, ch 1, (sc in next dc, ch 1, skip next dc) 3 times, sc in next 4 dc; repeat from ★ 4 times **more**, (ch 1, skip next dc, sc in next dc) 4 times; finish off: 72 sc and 48 ch-1 sps.
Row 7: With **right** side facing and holding 2 strands of Rust together, join yarn with slip st in first sc; ch 3, 2 dc in same st, ★ † (dc in next ch-1 sp and in next sc) 3 times, decrease, skip next 2 sc, decrease, (dc in next sc and in next ch-1 sp) 3 times †, (dc, ch 1, dc) in next 2 sc; repeat from ★ 4 times **more**, then repeat from † to † once, 3 dc in last sc: 110 dc and 10 ch-1 sps.
Row 8: Ch 3, turn; 2 dc in same st, dc in next 6 dc, decrease, skip next 2 dc, decrease, ★ dc in next 5 dc and in next ch-1 sp, (dc, ch 1, dc) in next 2 dc, dc in next ch-1 sp and in next 5 dc, decrease, skip next 2 dc, decrease; repeat from ★ 4 times **more**, dc in next 6 dc, 3 dc in last dc; finish off.
Rows 9-68: Repeat Rows 3-8, 10 times.

Holding fourteen 19" lengths of Rust together, add fringe in space at each point across short edges of Afghan *(Figs. 31a & c, page 143)*.

119

QUIET MOMENTS

The soothing shades of this handsome throw will beckon you to stay indoors and enjoy quiet moments. Puffy front post clusters add dimension to the jewel-tone stripes.

Finished Size: 50" x 71"

MATERIALS

Worsted Weight Yarn:
Ecru - 26 ounces, (740 grams, 1,785 yards)
Teal - 12¹/₂ ounces, (360 grams, 855 yards)
Red - 12 ounces, (340 grams, 825 yards)
Green - 12 ounces, (340 grams, 825 yards)
Crochet hook, size I (5.50 mm) **or** size needed for gauge

GAUGE: In pattern, 13 dc = 4"; 8 rows = 3³/₄"

Gauge Swatch: 5¹/₄"w x 4¹/₄"h
Ch 19 **loosely**.
Row 1: Dc in fourth ch from hook **(3 skipped chs count as first dc)** and in each ch across: 17 dc.
Work same as Afghan Rows 2-9.
Finish off.

STITCH GUIDE

FRONT POST CLUSTER *(abbreviated FP Cluster)*
Working in **front** of next ch-1, ★ YO, insert hook from **front** to **back** around post of skipped dc one row **below** ch-1 *(Fig. 9, page 139)*, YO and pull up a loop, YO and draw through 2 loops on hook; repeat from ★ 2 times **more**, YO and draw through all 4 loops on hook *(Fig. 15a, page 140)*.

AFGHAN BODY

With Teal, ch 163 **loosely**.
Row 1 (Right side)**:** Dc in fourth ch from hook **(3 skipped chs count as first dc)** and in each ch across: 161 dc.
Note: Loop a short piece of yarn around any stitch to mark Row 1 as **right** side.
Rows 2 and 3: Ch 3 **(counts as first dc, now and throughout)**, turn; dc in next dc and in each dc across.
Row 4: Ch 3, turn; dc in next 4 dc, ★ ch 1, skip next dc, dc in next 5 dc; repeat from ★ across changing to Ecru in last dc *(Fig. 27a, page 142)*: 135 dc and 26 ch-1 sps.

Row 5: Ch 1, turn; sc in first 5 dc, (work FP Cluster, sc in next 5 dc) across changing to Red in last sc: 26 FP Clusters and 135 sc.
Rows 6 and 7: Ch 3, turn; dc in next st and in each st across: 161 dc.
Row 8: Ch 3, turn; dc in next dc, ch 1, ★ skip next dc, dc in next 5 dc, ch 1; repeat from ★ across to last 3 dc, skip next dc, dc in last 2 dc changing to Ecru in last dc: 134 dc and 27 ch-1 sps.
Row 9: Ch 1, turn; sc in first 2 dc, work FP Cluster, (sc in next 5 dc, work FP Cluster) across to last 2 dc, sc in last 2 dc changing to Green in last sc: 27 FP Clusters and 134 sc.
Rows 10 and 11: Ch 3, turn; dc in next st and in each st across: 161 dc.
Row 12: Ch 3, turn; dc in next 4 dc, ★ ch 1, skip next dc, dc in next 5 dc; repeat from ★ across changing to Ecru in last dc: 135 dc and 26 ch-1 sps.
Row 13: Ch 1, turn; sc in first 5 dc, (work FP Cluster, sc in next 5 dc) across changing to Teal in last sc: 26 FP Clusters and 135 sc.
Rows 14-16: Repeat Rows 6-8.
Row 17: Ch 1, turn; sc in first 2 dc, work FP Cluster, (sc in next 5 dc, work FP Cluster) across to last 2 dc, sc in last 2 dc changing to Red in last sc: 27 FP Clusters and 134 sc.
Rows 18-20: Repeat Rows 10-12.
Row 21: Ch 1, turn; sc in first 5 dc, (work FP Cluster, sc in next 5 dc) across changing to Green in last sc: 26 FP Clusters and 135 sc.
Rows 22-24: Repeat Rows 6-8.
Row 25: Ch 1, turn; sc in first 2 dc, work FP Cluster, (sc in next 5 dc, work FP Cluster) across to last 2 dc, sc in last 2 dc changing to Teal in last sc: 27 FP Clusters and 134 sc.
Rows 26 and 27: Ch 3, turn; dc in next st and in each st across: 161 dc.
Rows 28-147: Repeat Rows 4-27, 5 times.
Rows 148 and 149: Ch 3, turn; dc in next st and in each st across.
Finish off.

EDGING

With **right** side facing, join Ecru with slip st in any st; ch 1, sc evenly around entire Afghan working 3 sc in each corner; join with slip st to first sc, finish off.

Holding 6 strands of Ecru together, add fringe evenly across short edges of Afghan *(Figs. 31a & c, page 143)*.

TUMBLEWEED

*If you love the look of the Southwest, this eye-catching throw
is for you! Crocheted in squares that reflect the colors of the desert,
the afghan has a playful pattern reminiscent of tumbleweeds.*

Finished Size: 47" x 64"

MATERIALS

Worsted Weight Yarn:

Tan - 32 ounces, (910 grams, 2,105 yards)
Lt Terra-Cotta - 6 ounces, (170 grams, 395 yards)
Black - 5 ounces, (140 grams, 330 yards)
Teal - 3 ounces, (90 grams, 195 yards)

Crochet hook, size I (5.50 mm) **or** size needed
for gauge
Yarn needle

GAUGE: Each Square = 5³/4"

SQUARE (Make 70)

Rnd 1 (Right side)**:** With Lt Terra-Cotta, ch 5, (dc, ch 1) 7
times in fifth ch from hook; join with slip st to fourth ch of
beginning ch-5, finish off: 8 ch-1 sps.

Note: Loop a short piece of yarn around any stitch to mark
Rnd 1 as **right** side.

Rnd 2: With **right** side facing, join Tan with slip st in any
ch-1 sp; ch 3 **(counts as first dc)**, 2 dc in same sp, (dc, ch 1,
tr, ch 1, dc) in next ch-1 sp, ★ 3 dc in next ch-1 sp, (dc, ch 1,
tr, ch 1, dc) in next ch-1 sp; repeat from ★ 2 times **more**; join
with slip st to first dc, finish off: 24 sts and 8 ch-1 sps.

Note: When working into a chain, insert hook under top loop
and the back ridge **(Fig. 2c, page 137)**.

Rnd 3: With **wrong** side facing, join Teal with sc in first ch to
left of any corner tr **(see Joining With Sc, page 142)**; ch 1,
skip next dc, (sc in next dc, ch 1, skip next dc) twice, sc in next
ch, ch 3, skip next tr, ★ sc in next ch, ch 1, skip next dc, (sc in
next dc, ch 1, skip next dc) twice, sc in next ch, ch 3, skip next
tr; repeat from ★ 2 times **more**; join with slip st to first sc,
finish off: 16 sc and 16 sps.

Rnd 4: With **right** side facing, join Tan with sc in first sc to left
of any corner ch-3 sp; ★ † (working **behind** next ch-1, dc in
dc one rnd **below** ch-1, sc in next sc) 3 times, working in **front**
of next ch-3, (dc, ch 1, tr, ch 1, dc) in tr one rnd **below** ch-3 †,
sc in next sc; repeat from ★ 2 times **more**, then repeat from
† to † once; join with slip st to first sc, finish off: 40 sts and
8 ch-1 sps.

Rnd 5: With **wrong** side facing, join Black with sc in first ch to
left of any corner tr; ★ † ch 1, skip next dc, (sc in next sc, ch 1,
skip next dc) across to first ch of next corner, sc in ch, ch 3,
skip next tr †, sc in next ch; repeat from ★ 2 times **more**, then
repeat from † to † once; join with slip st to first sc, finish off:
24 sc and 24 sps.

Rnd 6: With **right** side facing, join Tan with sc in first sc to left
of any corner ch-3 sp; ★ † (working **behind** next ch-1, dc in
dc one rnd **below** ch-1, sc in next sc) 5 times, working in **front**
of next ch-3, (dc, ch 1, tr, ch 1, dc) in tr one rnd **below** ch-3 †,
sc in next sc; repeat from ★ 2 times **more**, then repeat from
† to † once; join with slip st to first sc, finish off: 56 sts and
8 ch-1 sps.

Rnd 7: With Lt Terra-Cotta, repeat Rnd 5: 32 sc and 32 sps.

Rnd 8: With **right** side facing, join Tan with sc in first sc to left
of any corner ch-3 sp; ★ † working **behind** next ch-1, dc in dc
one rnd **below** ch-1, sc in next sc, working in **front** of next
ch-1, dc in dc one rnd **below** ch-1, sc in next sc, (working
behind next ch-1, dc in dc one rnd **below** ch-1, sc in next sc)
3 times, working in **front** of next ch-1, dc in dc one rnd **below**
ch-1, sc in next sc, working **behind** next ch-1, dc in dc one rnd
below ch-1, sc in next sc, working **behind** next ch-3, (dc,
ch 3, dc) in tr one rnd **below** ch-3 †, sc in next sc; repeat from
★ 2 times **more**, then repeat from † to † once; join with slip st
to first sc, finish off: 68 sts and 4 ch-3 sps.

Continued on page 124.

ASSEMBLY

With Tan and working through both loops, whipstitch Squares together *(Fig. 30b, page 143)*, forming 7 vertical strips of 10 Squares each, beginning in center ch of first corner ch-3 and ending in center ch of next corner ch-3; whipstitch strips together in same manner.

EDGING

Rnd 1: With **right** side facing, join Tan with sc in any corner ch-3 sp; ch 2, sc in same sp and in next 17 sts, (sc in next sp, hdc in joining, sc in next sp and in next 17 sts) across to next corner ch-3 sp, ★ (sc, ch 2, sc) in corner ch-3 sp, sc in next 17 sts, (sc in next sp, hdc in joining, sc in next sp and in next 17 sts) across to next corner ch-3 sp; repeat from ★ 2 times **more**; join with slip st to first sc, finish off: 676 sts and 4 ch-2 sps.

Rnd 2: With **wrong** side facing, join Black with sc in first sc to left of any corner ch-2 sp; ★ † (ch 1, skip next st, sc in next sc) across to next corner ch-2 sp, ch 3, skip corner ch-2 sp †, sc in next sc; repeat from ★ 2 times **more**, then repeat from † to † once; join with slip st to first sc, finish off: 340 sc and 340 sps.

Rnd 3: With **right** side facing, join Tan with sc in first sc to left of any corner ch-3 sp; ★ † working **behind** next ch-1, dc in sc one rnd **below** ch-1, sc in next sc, working in **front** of next ch-1, dc in sc one rnd **below** ch-1, sc in next sc, (working **behind** next ch-1, dc in sc one rnd **below** ch-1, sc in next sc) 5 times, working in **front** of next ch-1, dc in sc one rnd **below** ch-1, sc in next sc, [(working **behind** next ch-1, dc in st one rnd **below** ch-1, sc in next sc) 3 times, working in **front** of next ch-1, dc in sc one rnd **below** ch-1, sc in next sc, (working **behind** next ch-1, dc in sc one rnd **below** ch-1, sc in next sc) 5 times, working in **front** of next ch-1, dc in sc one rnd **below** ch-1, sc in next sc] across to within one ch-1 sp of next corner ch-3 sp, working **behind** next ch-1, dc in sc one rnd **below** ch-1, sc in next sc, working **behind** corner ch-3, (dc, ch 1, tr, ch 1, dc) in ch-2 sp one rnd **below** ch-3 †, sc in next sc; repeat from ★ 2 times **more**, then repeat from † to † once; join with slip st to first sc, finish off: 688 sts and 8 ch-1 sps.

Rnd 4: With **wrong** side facing, join Teal with sc in first ch to left of any corner tr; ★ † ch 1, skip next dc, (sc in next sc, ch 1, skip next dc) across to first ch of next corner, sc in ch, ch 3, skip next tr †, sc in next ch; repeat from ★ 2 times **more**, then repeat from † to † once; join with slip st to first sc, finish off: 348 sc and 348 sps.

Rnd 5: With **right** side facing, join Tan with sc in first sc to left of any corner ch-3 sp; ★ † (working **behind** next ch-1, dc in dc one rnd **below** ch-1, sc in next sc) twice, (working in **front** of next ch-1, dc in dc one rnd **below** ch-1, sc in next sc) twice, (working **behind** next ch-1, dc in dc one rnd **below** ch-1, sc in next sc) 3 times, [(working in **front** of next ch-1, dc in dc one rnd **below** ch-1, sc in next sc) 3 times, working **behind** next ch-1, dc in dc one rnd **below** ch-1, sc in next sc, (working in **front** of next ch-1, dc in dc one rnd **below** ch-1, sc in next sc) 3 times, (working **behind** next ch-1, dc in dc one rnd **below** ch-1, sc in next sc) 3 times] across to within 4 ch-1 sps of next corner ch-3 sp, (working in **front** of next ch-1, dc in dc one rnd **below** ch-1, sc in next sc) twice, (working **behind** next ch-1, dc in dc one rnd **below** ch-1, sc in next sc) twice, working **behind** corner ch-3, (dc, ch 1, tr, ch 1, dc) in tr one rnd **below** ch-3 †, sc in next sc; repeat from ★ 2 times **more**, then repeat from † to † once; join with slip st to first sc, finish off: 704 sts and 8 ch-1 sps.

Rnd 6: With Black, repeat Rnd 4: 356 sc and 356 sps.

Rnd 7: With **right** side facing, join Tan with sc in first sc to left of any corner ch-3 sp; ★ † (working **behind** next ch-1, dc in dc one rnd **below** ch-1, sc in next sc) 3 times, (working in **front** of next ch-1, dc in dc one rnd **below** ch-1, sc in next sc) twice, [working **behind** next ch-1, dc in dc one rnd **below** ch-1, sc in next sc, working in **front** of next ch-1, dc in dc one rnd **below** ch-1, sc in next sc, working **behind** next ch-1, dc in dc one rnd **below** ch-1, sc in next sc, (working in **front** of next ch-1, dc in dc one rnd **below** ch-1, sc in next sc) twice] across to within 3 ch-1 sps of next corner ch-3 sp, (working **behind** next ch-1, dc in dc one rnd **below** ch-1, sc in next sc) 3 times, working **behind** corner ch-3, (dc, ch 1, tr, ch 1, dc) in tr one rnd **below** ch-3 †, sc in next sc; repeat from ★ 2 times **more**, then repeat from † to † once; join with slip st to first sc, finish off: 720 sts and 8 ch-1 sps.

Rnd 8: Repeat Rnd 4: 364 sc and 364 sps.

Rnd 9: With **right** side facing, join Tan with sc in first sc to left of any corner ch-3 sp; ★ † (working **behind** next ch-1, dc in dc one rnd **below** ch-1, sc in next sc) 4 times, (working in **front** of next ch-1, dc in dc one rnd **below** ch-1, sc in next sc) twice, (working **behind** next ch-1, dc in dc one rnd **below** ch-1, sc in next sc) 3 times, [(working in **front** of next ch-1, dc in dc one rnd **below** ch-1, sc in next sc) 3 times, working **behind** next ch-1, dc in dc one rnd **below** ch-1, sc in next sc, (working in **front** of next ch-1, dc in dc one rnd **below** ch-1, sc in next sc) 3 times, (working **behind** next ch-1, dc in dc one rnd **below** ch-1, sc in next sc) 3 times] across to within 6 ch-1 sps of next corner ch-3 sp, (working in **front** of next ch-1, dc in dc one rnd **below** ch-1, sc in next sc) twice, (working **behind** next ch-1, dc in dc one rnd **below** ch-1, sc in next sc) 4 times, working **behind** corner ch-3, (dc, ch 1, tr, ch 1, dc) in tr one rnd **below** ch-3 †, sc in next sc; repeat from ★ 2 times **more**, then repeat from † to † once; join with slip st to first sc, finish off: 736 sts and 8 ch-1 sps.

Rnd 10: With Black, repeat Rnd 4: 372 sc and 372 sps.

Rnd 11: With **right** side facing, join Tan with sc in first sc to left of any corner ch-3 sp; ★ † [(working **behind** next ch-1, dc in dc one rnd **below** ch-1, sc in next sc) 5 times, working in **front** of next ch-1, dc in dc one rnd **below** ch-1, sc in next sc] twice, [(working **behind** next ch-1, dc in dc one rnd **below** ch-1, sc in next sc) 3 times, working in **front** of next ch-1, dc in dc one rnd **below** ch-1, sc in next sc, (working **behind** next ch-1, dc in dc one rnd **below** ch-1, sc in next sc) 5 times, working in **front** of next ch-1, dc in dc one rnd **below** ch-1, sc in next sc] across to within 5 ch-1 sps of next corner ch-3 sp, (working **behind** next ch-1, dc in dc one rnd **below** ch-1, sc in next sc) 5 times, working **behind** corner ch-3, (dc, ch 1, tr, ch 1, dc) in tr one rnd **below** ch-3 †, sc in next sc; repeat from ★ 2 times **more**, then repeat from † to † once; join with slip st to first sc, do **not** finish off: 752 sts and 8 ch-1 sps.

Rnd 12: Ch 2, skip next dc, ★ (slip st in next sc, ch 2, skip next dc) across to first ch-1 sp of next corner, slip st in ch-1 sp, ch 3, skip next tr, slip st in next ch-1 sp, ch 2, skip next dc; repeat from ★ around; join with slip st to first slip st, finish off.

YULETIDE BLOCKS

For a joyous holiday, wrap a loved one in this Yuletide throw! The afghan works up quickly holding two strands of yarn, and vertical lines of slip stitches are then added to create the cheery blocks.

Finished Size: 46" x 67"

MATERIALS
Worsted Weight Yarn:
Red - 17¹/₂ ounces,
(500 grams, 1,100 yards)
Green - 14¹/₂ ounces,
(410 grams, 910 yards)
Ecru - 11 ounces,
(310 grams, 690 yards)
Crochet hook, size Q (15.00 mm)

Note: Entire Afghan is worked holding two strands of yarn together.

GAUGE: In pattern, 11 sts and 11 rows = 7"

Gauge Swatch: 7" square
With Red, ch 12 **loosely**.
Work same as Afghan for 11 rows.

AFGHAN BODY
With Red, ch 72 **loosely**.

Row 1 (Right side)**:** Sc in second ch from hook and in next 4 chs, (ch 1, skip next ch, sc in next 5 chs) across: 60 sc and 11 ch-1 sps.

Note: Loop a short piece of yarn around any stitch to mark Row 1 as **right** side and bottom edge.

Row 2: Ch 1, turn; sc in first 5 sc, (ch 1, sc in next 5 sc) across.

Row 3: Ch 1, turn; sc in first 5 sc, (ch 1, sc in next 5 sc) across; finish off.

Row 4: With **right** side facing and working in Back Loops Only *(Fig. 25, page 142)*, join Ecru with sc in first sc *(see Joining with Sc, page 142)*; sc in next 4 sc, (ch 1, sc in next 5 sc) across; finish off.

Row 5: With **right** side facing and working in Back Loops Only, join Red with sc in first sc; sc in next 4 sc, (ch 1, sc in next 5 sc) across.

Row 6: Ch 1, turn; working in both loops, sc in first 5 sc, (ch 1, sc in next 5 sc) across.

Row 7: Ch 1, turn; sc in first 5 sc, (ch 1, sc in next 5 sc) across; finish off.

Row 8: With **right** side facing and working in Back Loops Only, join Green with sc in first sc; sc in next 4 sc, (ch 1, sc in next 5 sc) across.

Row 9: Ch 1, turn; working in both loops, sc in first 5 sc, (ch 1, sc in next 5 sc) across.

Row 10: Ch 1, turn; sc in first 5 sc, (ch 1, sc in next 5 sc) across; finish off.

Row 11: With **right** side facing and working in Back Loops Only, join Ecru with sc in first sc; sc in next 4 sc, (ch 1, sc in next 5 sc) across; finish off.

Rows 12-14: Repeat Rows 8-10.

Rows 15-17: Repeat Rows 5-7.

Rows 18-105: Repeat Rows 4-17, 6 times; then repeat Rows 4-7 once **more**.

VERTICAL STRIPES

Note: Keep working yarn on **wrong** side of Afghan.

With **right** side facing and Ecru, insert hook in any ch-1 sp on Row 1 and pull up a loop, working vertically, ★ insert hook in next ch-1 sp in row above, YO and draw **loosely** through loop on hook; repeat from ★ across to top; finish off.

Repeat for remaining 10 Vertical Stripes.

EDGING

With **right** side facing, join Ecru with slip st in any st; ch 1, sc evenly around entire Afghan working 3 sc in each corner; join with slip st to first sc, finish off.

CHRISTMAS DAZZLE

Dazzle that special someone on your gift list with this cozy coverlet. Fashioned in the traditional colors of Christmas, the afghan features an elegant pattern of jewel-like clusters.

Finished Size: 47" x 60"

MATERIALS

Worsted Weight Yarn:

Ecru - 27¹/₂ ounces, (780 grams, 1,805 yards)

Red - 9¹/₂ ounces, (270 grams, 625 yards)

Green - 9¹/₂ ounces, (270 grams, 625 yards)

Crochet hook, size J (6.00 mm) **or** size needed for gauge

GAUGE: In pattern, (5 dc, sc) twice and 6 rows = 3¹/₄"

Gauge Swatch: 6¹/₂" square

With Ecru, ch 28 **loosely**.

Work same as Afghan for 12 rows.

Finish off.

STITCH GUIDE

> **CLUSTER** (uses next 5 sts)
>
> ★ YO, insert hook in **next** st, YO and pull up a loop, YO and draw through 2 loops on hook; repeat from ★ 4 times **more**, YO and draw through all 6 loops on hook *(Fig. 15b, page 140)*.

AFGHAN BODY

With Ecru, ch 172 **loosely**.

Row 1 (Right side)**:** 2 Dc in fourth ch from hook **(3 skipped chs count as first dc)**, skip next 2 chs, sc in next ch, ★ skip next 2 chs, 5 dc in next ch, skip next 2 chs, sc in next ch; repeat from ★ across to last 3 chs, skip next 2 chs, 3 dc in last ch changing to Red in last dc *(Fig. 27a, page 142)*: 169 sts.

Note: Loop a short piece of yarn around any stitch to mark Row 1 as **right** side.

Row 2: Ch 1, turn; sc in first dc, ★ ch 2, work Cluster, ch 2, sc in next dc; repeat from ★ across changing to Ecru in last sc: 28 Clusters.

Row 3: Ch 3 **(counts as first dc, now and throughout)**, turn; 2 dc in same st, sc in next Cluster, ★ 5 dc in next sc, sc in next Cluster; repeat from ★ across to last sc, 3 dc in last sc changing to Green in last dc: 169 sts.

Row 4: Ch 1, turn; sc in first dc, ★ ch 2, work Cluster, ch 2, sc in next dc; repeat from ★ across changing to Ecru in last sc: 28 Clusters.

Row 5: Ch 3, turn; 2 dc in same st, sc in next Cluster, ★ 5 dc in next sc, sc in next Cluster; repeat from ★ across to last sc, 3 dc in last sc changing to Red in last dc: 169 sts.

Row 6: Ch 1, turn; sc in first dc, ★ ch 2, work Cluster, ch 2, sc in next dc; repeat from ★ across changing to Ecru in last sc: 28 Clusters.

Row 7: Ch 3, turn; 2 dc in same st, sc in next Cluster, ★ 5 dc in next sc, sc in next Cluster; repeat from ★ across to last sc, 3 dc in last sc changing to Green in last dc: 169 sts.

Repeat Rows 4-7 until Afghan measures approximately 60" from beginning ch, ending by working Row 7, do **not** change colors.

EDGING

Ch 1, do **not** turn; sc evenly around entire Afghan working 3 sc in each corner; join with slip st to first sc, finish off.

Holding 4 strands of Ecru together, add fringe in every other st across short edges of Afghan *(Figs. 31a & c, page 143)*.

129

FIT FOR A KING

*Rich and luxurious — these attributes make this regal afghan
fit for a king! It's the perfect Christmas gift for a favorite gentleman.*

Finished Size: 45" x 66"

MATERIALS
Worsted Weight Yarn:
  Blue - 21 ounces, (600 grams, 1,380 yards)
  Green - 12 ounces, (340 grams, 790 yards)
  Variegated - 9 ounces, (260 grams, 415 yards)
Crochet hook, size G (4.00 mm) **or** size needed
  for gauge

GAUGE: Each Square = 10¹⁄₂"

Gauge Swatch: 7¹⁄₂"
Work same as Center.

STITCH GUIDE

REVERSE SINGLE CROCHET *(abbreviated reverse sc)*
Working from **left** to **right**, insert hook in hdc to right of
hook, YO and draw through, under, and to left of loop on
hook (2 loops on hook), YO and draw through both loops on
hook **(reverse sc made, *Figs. 23a-d, page 141)*.

SQUARE (Make 24)
CENTER
With Blue, ch 31 **loosely**.

Row 1 (Right side)**:** Sc in second ch from hook and in each ch
across: 30 sc.
Note: Loop a short piece of yarn around any stitch to mark
Row 1 as **right** side and bottom edge.
Row 2: Ch 4 **(counts as first dc plus ch 1, now and
throughout)**, ★ skip next sc, dc in next 2 sc, ch 1; repeat from
★ across to last 2 sc, skip next sc, dc in last sc: 20 dc and
10 ch-1 sps.
Row 3: Ch 1, turn; sc in each dc and in each ch-1 sp across:
30 sc.
Rows 4-21: Repeat Rows 2 and 3, 9 times.
Finish off.

BORDER
Rnd 1: With **right** side of Center facing, join Green with slip st
in first sc on Row 21; ch 3 **(counts as first dc, now and
throughout)**, 2 dc in same st, dc in each sc across to last sc,
3 dc in last sc; work 28 dc evenly spaced across end of rows;
working in free loops of beginning ch *(Fig. 26b, page 142)*,
3 dc in first ch, dc in next 28 chs, 3 dc in next ch; work 28 dc
evenly spaced across end of rows; join with slip st to first dc,
finish off: 124 dc.
Rnd 2: With **right** side facing, join Variegated with slip st in any
dc; ch 3, dc in each dc around working 3 dc in center dc of
each corner; join with slip st to first dc, finish off: 132 dc.
Rnd 3: With Green, repeat Rnd 2: 140 dc.

ASSEMBLY
Afghan is assembled by joining Squares together, forming
4 vertical strips of 6 Squares each, and then joining strips.
Join Squares as follows: With **right** sides together, matching top
edge of one Square to bottom edge of next Square, and working
through **both** loops on **both** pieces, join Blue with slip st in
center dc of first corner; ch 1, sc in same st and in each dc
across to center dc of next corner, sc in center dc; finish off.
Join strips together in same manner.

EDGING
Rnd 1: With **right** side facing, join Green with slip st in center
dc of top right corner; ch 1, 2 sc in same st, † sc in each dc and
in each joining across to center dc of next corner, 3 sc in center
dc, skip next dc, sc in each dc and in each joining across to
center dc of next corner †, 3 sc in center dc, repeat from † to †
once, sc in same st as first sc; join with slip st to first sc, do **not**
finish off: 706 sc.

Continued on page 135.

SNOWFLAKES

Created in colors that bring to mind snowy landscapes and majestic evergreens, this Nordic-inspired throw has an intricate pattern of snowflakes. What a great way to bring a winter wonderland indoors!

Finished Size: 51" x 67"

MATERIALS

Worsted Weight Yarn:

White - 39 ounces, (1,110 grams, 2,460 yards)

Green - 27 ounces, (770 grams, 1,700 yards)

Crochet hook, size I (5.50 mm) or size needed for gauge

GAUGE: 14 sc and 16 rows = 4"

Gauge Swatch: 8³⁄₄"w x 4"h

With Green, ch 32 **loosely**.

Work same as Afghan for 16 rows.

Finish off.

AFGHAN BODY

With Green, ch 176 **loosely**.

Row 1: Sc in second ch from hook, (ch 1, skip next ch, sc in next ch) across changing to White in last sc *(Fig. 27a, page 142)*: 88 sc and 87 ch-1 sps.

Row 2 (Right side): Ch 1, turn; sc in first sc, (ch 1, sc in next sc) across changing to Green in last sc.

Row 3: Ch 1, turn; sc in first sc, ★ working **behind** next ch-1, dc in ch-1 sp one row **below** ch-1, sc in next sc; repeat from ★ across changing to White in last sc: 175 sts.

Row 4: Ch 1, turn; sc in each st across changing to Green in last sc.

Row 5: Ch 1, turn; sc in first 2 sc, ch 1, (skip next sc, sc in next sc, ch 1) across to last 3 sc, skip next sc, sc in last 2 sc changing to White in last sc: 89 sc and 86 ch-1 sps.

Row 6: Ch 1, turn; sc in first 2 sc, ★ † (working in **front** of next ch-1, dc in sc one row **below** ch-1, sc in next sc) twice, working **behind** next ch-1, dc in sc one row **below** ch-1 †, sc in next sc; repeat from ★ across to last 6 sc, then repeat from † to † once, (sc in next sc, working in **front** of next ch-1, dc in sc one row **below** ch-1) twice, sc in last 2 sc changing to Green in last sc: 175 sts.

Row 7: Ch 1, turn; sc in first 2 sc, ★ † (ch 1, skip next dc, sc in next sc) twice, working **behind** next dc, dc in ch-1 sp one row **below** dc †, sc in next sc; repeat from ★ across to last 11 sts, then repeat from † to † once, (sc in next sc, ch 1, skip next dc) twice, sc in last 2 sc changing to White in last sc: 117 sts and 58 ch-1 sps.

Row 8: Ch 1, turn; sc in first 2 sc, working in **front** of next ch-1, dc in dc one row **below** ch-1, sc in next sc, working in **front** of next ch-1, dc in dc one row **below** ch-1, ★ sc in next 3 sts, working in **front** of next ch-1, dc in dc one row **below** ch-1, sc in next sc, working in **front** of next ch-1, dc in dc one row **below** ch-1; repeat from ★ across to last 2 sc, sc in last 2 sc changing to Green in last sc: 175 sts.

Row 9: Ch 1, turn; sc in first sc, (ch 1, skip next sc, sc in next st) across changing to White in last sc: 88 sc and 87 ch-1 sps.

Row 10: Ch 1, turn; sc in first sc, ★ working **behind** next ch-1, dc in sc one row **below** ch-1, sc in next sc; repeat from ★ across changing to Green in last sc: 175 sts.

Row 11: Ch 1, turn; sc in first sc, ★ working **behind** next dc, dc in ch-1 sp one row **below** dc, sc in next sc; repeat from ★ across changing to White in last sc.

Row 12: Ch 1, turn; sc in each st across changing to Green in last sc.

Row 13: Ch 1, turn; sc in first sc, (ch 1, skip next sc, sc in next sc) twice, ★ † ch 2, skip next 2 sc, sc in next sc, ch 3, skip next 3 sc, sc in next sc, ch 2, skip next 2 sc, sc in next sc †, ch 1, skip next sc, sc in next sc; repeat from ★ across to last 14 sc, then repeat from † to † once, (ch 1, skip next sc, sc in next sc) twice changing to White in last sc: 60 sc and 59 sps.

Row 14: Ch 1, turn; sc in first sc, working in **front** of next ch-1, dc in sc one row **below** ch-1, sc in next sc, working **behind** next ch-1, dc in sc one row **below** ch-1, sc in next sc, ★ working in **front** of next ch-2, dc in next 2 sc one row **below** ch-2, sc in next sc, working in **front** of next ch-3, dc in next 3 sc one row **below** ch-3, sc in next sc, working in **front** of next ch-2, dc in next 2 sc one row **below** ch-2, sc in next sc, working **behind** next ch-1, dc in sc one row **below** ch-1, sc in next sc; repeat from ★ across to last ch-1, working in **front** of last ch-1, dc in sc one row **below** ch-1, sc in last sc changing to Green: 175 sts.

Continued on page 134.

Row 15: Ch 1, turn; sc in first sc, ch 1, skip next dc, sc in next sc, working **behind** next dc, dc in ch-1 sp one row **below** dc, sc in next sc, ★ (ch 1, skip next st, sc in next st) 5 times, working **behind** next dc, dc in ch-1 sp one row **below** dc, sc in next sc; repeat from ★ across to last 2 sts, ch 1, skip next dc, sc in last sc changing to White: 103 sts and 72 ch-1 sps.

Row 16: Ch 1, turn; sc in first sc, working in **front** of next ch-1, dc in dc one row **below** ch-1, sc in next 3 sts, working in **front** of next ch-1, dc in dc one row **below** ch-1, ★ (sc in next sc, working **behind** next ch-1, dc in sc one row **below** ch-1, sc in next sc, working in **front** of next ch-1, dc in dc one row **below** ch-1) twice, sc in next 3 sts, working in **front** of next ch-1, dc in dc one row **below** ch-1; repeat from ★ across to last sc, sc in last sc changing to Green: 175 sts.

Row 17: Ch 1, turn; sc in first sc, (ch 2, skip next 2 sts, sc in next sc) twice, ★ working **behind** next dc, dc in ch-1 sp one row **below** dc, sc in next sc, ch 1, skip next dc, sc in next sc, working **behind** next dc, dc in ch-1 sp one row **below** dc, sc in next sc, (ch 2, skip next 2 sts, sc in next sc) twice; repeat from ★ across changing to White in last sc: 101 sts and 44 sps.

Row 18: Ch 1, turn; sc in first sc, working in **front** of next ch-2, dc in next 2 sts one row **below** ch-2, sc in next sc, working in **front** of next ch-2, dc in next 2 sts one row **below** ch-2, ★ sc in next 3 sts, working **behind** next ch-1, dc in dc one row **below** ch-1, sc in next 3 sts, working in **front** of next ch-2, dc in next 2 sts one row **below** ch-2, sc in next sc, working in **front** of next ch-2, dc in next 2 sts one row **below** ch-2; repeat from ★ across to last sc, sc in last sc changing to Green: 175 sts.

Row 19: Ch 1, turn; sc in first sc, (ch 2, skip next 2 dc, sc in next sc) twice, ★ ch 1, skip next sc, sc in next sc, working **behind** next dc, dc in ch-1 sp one row **below** dc, sc in next sc, ch 1, skip next sc, sc in next sc, (ch 2, skip next 2 dc, sc in next sc) twice; repeat from ★ across changing to White in last sc: 87 sts and 58 sps.

Row 20: Ch 1, turn; sc in first sc, (working in **front** of next ch-2, dc in next 2 dc one row **below** ch-2, sc in next sc) twice, ★ working **behind** next ch-1, dc in sc one row **below** ch-1, sc in next 3 sts, working **behind** next ch-1, dc in sc one row **below** ch-1, sc in next sc, (working in **front** of next ch-2, dc in next 2 dc one row **below** ch-2, sc in next sc) twice; repeat from ★ across changing to Green in last sc: 175 sts.

Row 21: Ch 1, turn; sc in first sc, (ch 1, skip next st, sc in next st) 3 times, ★ working **behind** next dc, dc in ch-1 sp one row **below** dc, sc in next sc, ch 1, skip next sc, sc in next sc, working **behind** next dc, dc in ch-1 sp one row **below** dc, sc in next sc, (ch 1, skip next st, sc in next st) 3 times; repeat from ★ across changing to White in last sc: 116 sts and 59 ch-1 sps.

Row 22: Ch 1, turn; sc in first sc, working in **front** of next ch-1, dc in dc one row **below** ch-1, sc in next sc, working **behind** next ch-1, dc in sc one row **below** ch-1, sc in next sc, working in **front** of next ch-1, dc in dc one row **below** ch-1, ★ (sc in next 3 sts, working in **front** of next ch-1, dc in st one row **below** ch-1) twice, sc in next sc, working **behind** next ch-1, dc in sc one row **below** ch-1, sc in next sc, working in **front** of next ch-1, dc in dc one row **below** ch-1; repeat from ★ across to last sc, sc in last sc changing to Green: 175 sts.

Row 23: Ch 1, turn; sc in first sc, ch 1, skip next dc, sc in next sc, working **behind** next dc, dc in ch-1 sp one row **below** dc, sc in next sc, ★ ch 2, skip next 2 sts, sc in next sc, ch 3, skip next 3 sts, sc in next sc, ch 2, skip next 2 sts, sc in next sc, working **behind** next dc, dc in ch-1 sp one row **below** dc, sc in next sc; repeat from ★ across to last 2 sts, ch 1, skip next dc, sc in last sc changing to White: 75 sts and 44 sps.

Row 24: Ch 1, turn; sc in first sc, working in **front** of next ch-1, dc in dc one row **below** ch-1, sc in next 3 sts, ★ working in **front** of next ch-2, dc in next 2 sts one row **below** ch-2, sc in next sc, working in **front** of next ch-3, dc in next 3 sts one row **below** ch-3, sc in next sc, working in **front** of next ch-2, dc in next 2 sts one row **below** ch-2, sc in next 3 sts; repeat from ★ across to last ch-1, working in **front** of last ch-1, dc in dc one row **below** ch-1, sc in last sc changing to Green: 175 sts.

Row 25: Ch 1, turn; sc in first sc, (ch 1, skip next st, sc in next st) across changing to White in last sc: 88 sc and 87 ch-1 sps.

Rows 26-36: Repeat Rows 2-12.

Row 37: Ch 1, turn; sc in first 2 sts, ch 3, (skip next 3 sts, sc in next st, ch 3) across to last 5 sts, skip next 3 sts, sc in last 2 sts changing to White in last sc: 46 sc and 43 ch-3 sps.

Row 38: Ch 1, turn; sc in first 2 sc, working in **front** of next ch-3, dc in next 3 sts one row **below** ch-3, ★ sc in next sc, working in **front** of next ch-3, dc in next 3 sts one row **below** ch-3; repeat from ★ across to last 2 sc, sc in last 2 sc changing to Green in last sc: 175 sts.

Row 39: Ch 1, turn; sc in first sc, ch 2, skip next 2 sts, sc in next dc, (ch 3, skip next 3 sts, sc in next dc) across to last 3 sts, ch 2, skip next 2 sts, sc in last sc changing to White: 45 sc and 44 sps.

Row 40: Ch 1, turn; sc in first sc, working in **front** of next ch-2, dc in next 2 sts one row **below** ch-2, sc in next sc, ★ working in **front** of next ch-3, dc in next 3 sts one row **below** ch-3, sc in next sc; repeat from ★ across to last ch-2, working in **front** of last ch-2, dc in next 2 sts one row **below** ch-2, sc in last sc changing to Green: 175 sts.

Rows 41-46: Repeat Rows 37-40 once, then repeat Rows 37 and 38 once **more**.

Row 47: Ch 1, turn; sc in first sc, (ch 1, skip next st, sc in next st) across changing to White in last sc: 88 sc and 89 ch-1 sps.

Rows 48-265: Repeat Rows 2-47, 4 times; then repeat Rows 2-35 once **more**; at end of last row, do **not** change colors.

EDGING

Ch 3, turn; dc evenly around entire Afghan working 3 dc in each corner; join with slip st to top of beginning ch-3, finish off.

FIT FOR A KING Continued from page 130.

Continued from page 130.

Rnd 2: Ch 2 (**counts as first hdc, now and throughout**), 2 hdc in same st changing to Blue in last hdc, do **not** cut Green **(Fig. 27a, page 142)**, hdc in next 3 sc, (with Green hdc in next 3 sc, with Blue hdc in next 3 sc) across to center sc of next corner, with Green 3 hdc in center sc, (with Blue hdc in next 3 sc, with Green hdc in next 3 sc) across to center sc of next corner, with Blue 3 hdc in center sc, with Green hdc in next 3 sc, (with Blue hdc in next 3 sc, with Green hdc in next 3 sc) across to center sc of next corner, with Blue 3 hdc in center sc, (with Green hdc in next 3 sc, with Blue hdc in next 3 sc) across; join with slip st to first hdc; cut Green.

Rnd 3: Ch 2, hdc in each hdc around working 3 hdc in center hdc of each corner; join with slip st to first hdc.

Rnd 4: Ch 2, **turn**; hdc in each hdc around working 3 hdc in center hdc of each corner; join with slip st to first hdc.

Rnd 5: Ch 1, **turn**; work reverse sc in each hdc around; join with slip st to first st, finish off.

general instructions

BASIC INFORMATION

ABBREVIATIONS

BPdc	Back Post double crochet(s)
ch(s)	chain(s)
dc	double crochet(s)
Dk	Dark
dtr	double treble crochet(s)
FP	Front Post
FPdc	Front Post double crochet(s)
FPdtr	Front Post double treble crochet(s)
FPsc	Front Post single crochet(s)
FPtr	Front Post treble crochet(s)
hdc	half double crochet(s)
LDC	Long double crochet(s)
LFP	Long Front Post
LHDC	Long half double crochet(s)
LSC	Long single crochet(s)
Lt	Light
mm	millimeters
Rnd(s)	Round(s)
sc	single crochet(s)
sp(s)	space(s)
st(s)	stitch(es)
tr	treble crochet(s)
YO	yarn over

SYMBOLS

★ — work instructions following ★ as many **more** times as indicated in addition to the first time.

† to † — work all instructions from first † to second † **as many** times as specified.

( ) or [ ] — work enclosed instructions **as many** times as specified by the number immediately following **or** work all enclosed instructions in the stitch or space indicated **or** contains explanatory remarks.

colon (:) — the number(s) given after a colon at the end of a row or round denote(s) the number of stitches you should have on that row or round.

TERMS

chain loosely — work the chain **only** loose enough for the hook to pass through the chain easily when working the next row or round into the chain.

multiple — the number of stitches required to complete one repeat of a pattern.

post — the vertical shaft of a stitch.

right side vs. wrong side — the right side of your work is the side that will show when the piece is finished.

work across or around — continue working in the established pattern.

GAUGE

Gauge is the number of stitches and rows or rounds per inch and is used to determine the finished size of a project. All crochet patterns specify the gauge that you must match to ensure proper size and to ensure that you will have enough yarn to complete the project.

Hook size given in instructions is merely a guide. Because everyone crochets differently — loosely, tightly, or somewhere in between — the finished size can vary, even when crocheters use the very same pattern, yarn, and hook.

Before beginning any crocheted item, it is absolutely necessary for you to crochet a gauge swatch in the pattern stitch indicated and with the weight of yarn and hook size suggested. Your swatch must be large enough to measure your gauge. Lay your swatch on a hard, smooth, flat surface. Then measure it, counting your stitches and rows or rounds carefully. If your swatch is smaller than specified or you have too many stitches per inch, try again with a larger size hook; if your swatch is larger than specified or you don't have enough stitches per inch, try again with a smaller size hook. Keep trying until you find the size that will give you the specified gauge. DO NOT HESITATE TO CHANGE HOOK SIZE TO OBTAIN CORRECT GAUGE. Once proper gauge is obtained, measure width of piece approximately every 3" to be sure gauge remains consistent.

BASIC STITCH GUIDE

CHAIN *(abbreviated ch)*

To work a chain stitch, begin with a slip knot on the hook. Bring the yarn **over** hook from **back** to **front**, catching the yarn with the hook and turning the hook slightly toward you to keep the yarn from slipping off. Draw the yarn through the slip knot *(Fig. 1)*.

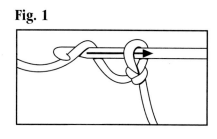

Fig. 1

WORKING INTO THE CHAIN

When beginning a first row of crochet in a chain, always skip the first chain from the hook and work into the second chain from hook (for single crochet), third chain from hook (for half double crochet), or fourth chain from hook (for double crochet), etc. *(Fig. 2a)*.

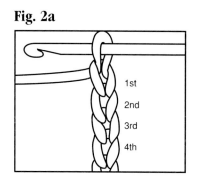

Fig. 2a

1st
2nd
3rd
4th

Method 1: Insert hook into back ridge of each chain indicated *(Fig. 2b)*.
Method 2: Insert hook under top loop **and** the back ridge of each chain indicated *(Fig. 2c)*.

Fig. 2b

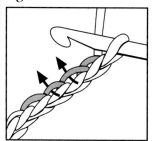

Fig. 2c

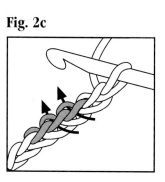

SLIP STITCH *(abbreviated slip st)*

This stitch is used to attach new yarn, to join work, or to move the yarn across a group of stitches without adding height. Insert hook in stitch or space indicated, YO and draw through stitch **and** loop on hook *(Fig. 3)*.

Fig. 3

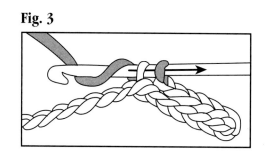

SINGLE CROCHET *(abbreviated sc)*

Insert hook in stitch or space indicated, YO and pull up a loop, YO and draw through both loops on hook *(Fig. 4)*.

Fig. 4

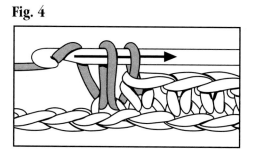

HALF DOUBLE CROCHET
(abbreviated hdc)

YO, insert hook in stitch or space indicated, YO and pull up a loop, YO and draw through all 3 loops on hook *(Fig. 5)*.

Fig. 5

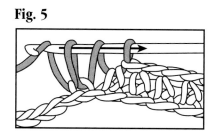

137

DOUBLE CROCHET *(abbreviated dc)*

YO, insert hook in stitch or space indicated, YO and pull up a loop (3 loops on hook), YO and draw through 2 loops on hook *(Fig. 6a)*, YO and draw through remaining 2 loops on hook *(Fig. 6b)*.

Fig. 6a

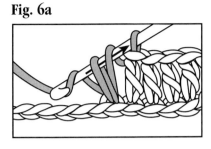

Fig. 6b

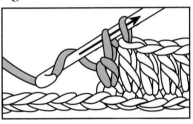

TREBLE CROCHET *(abbreviated tr)*

YO twice, insert hook in stitch or space indicated, YO and pull up a loop (4 loops on hook) *(Fig. 7a)*, (YO and draw through 2 loops on hook) 3 times *(Fig. 7b)*.

Fig. 7a

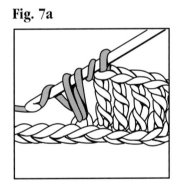

Fig. 7b

DOUBLE TREBLE CROCHET *(abbreviated dtr)*

YO 3 times, insert hook in stitch or space indicated, YO and pull up a loop (5 loops on hook) *(Fig. 8a)*, (YO and draw through 2 loops on hook) 4 times *(Fig. 8b)*.

Fig. 8a

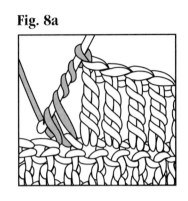

Fig. 8b

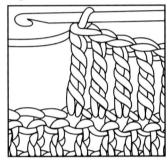

PATTERN STITCHES

POST STITCH

Work around post of stitch indicated, inserting hook in direction of arrow *(Fig. 9)*.

Fig. 9

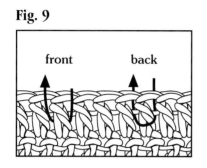

FRONT POST SINGLE CROCHET
(abbreviated FPsc)

Insert hook from **front** to **back** around post of stitch indicated *(Fig. 9)*, YO and pull up a loop *(Fig. 10)*, YO and draw through both loops on hook.

Fig. 10

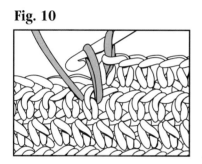

FRONT POST DOUBLE CROCHET
(abbreviated FPdc)

YO, insert hook from **front** to **back** around post of stitch indicated *(Fig. 9)*, YO and pull up a loop (3 loops on hook) *(Fig. 11)*, (YO and draw through 2 loops on hook) twice.

Fig. 11

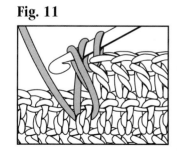

FRONT POST TREBLE CROCHET
(abbreviated FPtr)

YO twice, insert hook from **front** to **back** around post of stitch indicated *(Fig. 9)*, YO and pull up a loop (4 loops on hook) *(Fig. 12)*, (YO and draw through 2 loops on hook) 3 times.

Fig. 12

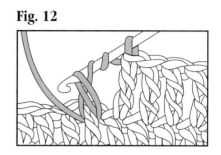

FRONT POST DOUBLE TREBLE CROCHET *(abbreviated FPdtr)*

YO 3 times, insert hook from **front** to **back** around post of stitch indicated *(Fig. 9)*, YO and pull up a loop (5 loops on hook) *(Fig. 13)*, (YO and draw through 2 loops on hook) 4 times.

Fig. 13

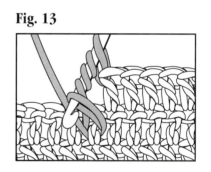

BACK POST DOUBLE CROCHET
(abbreviated BPdc)

YO, insert hook from **back** to **front** around post of stitch indicated *(Fig. 9)*, YO and pull up a loop (3 loops on hook) *(Fig. 14)*, (YO and draw through 2 loops on hook) twice.

Fig. 14

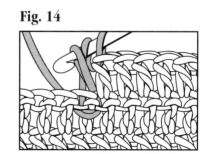

CLUSTER

A Cluster can be worked all in the same stitch or space *(Fig. 15a)*, **or** across several stitches *(Fig. 15b)*.

Fig. 15a

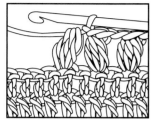

Fig. 15b

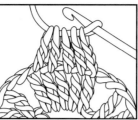

FRONT POST DOUBLE CROCHET CLUSTER
(abbreviated FPdc Cluster)

★ YO, insert hook from **front** to **back** around **next** leg of tr Cluster *(Fig. 16)*, YO and pull up a loop, YO and draw through 2 loops on hook; repeat from ★ 3 times **more**, YO and draw through all 5 loops on hook. Skip tr Cluster behind FPdc Cluster.

Fig. 16

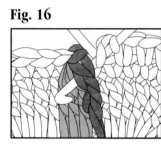

LONG FRONT POST CLUSTER
(abbreviated LFP Cluster)

YO 5 times, insert hook from **front** to **back** around post of dc **before** corner ch-2 sp on Rnd 1 *(Fig. 17a)*, YO and pull up a loop, (YO and draw through 2 loops on hook) 5 times, YO 5 times, insert hook from **front** to **back** around post of dc **after** same corner ch-2 sp on Rnd 1 *(Fig. 17b)*, YO and pull up a loop, (YO and draw through 2 loops on hook) 5 times, YO and draw through all 3 loops on hook.

Fig. 17a

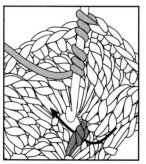

Fig. 17b

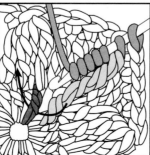

SPLIT TREBLE CROCHET
(abbreviated Split tr)

YO twice, working in **front** of last 3 dc made, insert hook from **back** to **front** in free loop just created on Rnd 5 *(Fig. 18a)*, YO and pull up a loop, (YO and draw through 2 loops on hook) twice, YO twice, skip next 2 sc, insert hook from **front** to **back** in Front Loop Only of next sc *(Fig. 18b)*, YO and pull up a loop, (YO and draw through 2 loops on hook) twice, YO and draw through all 3 loops on hook.

Fig. 18a

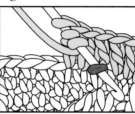

Fig. 18b

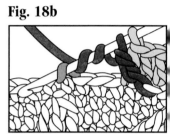

SPLIT TREBLE CROCHET CLUSTER
(abbreviated Split tr Cluster)

YO twice, working in **front** of last 3 dc made, insert hook from **back** to **front** in center of same Split tr as last tr made *(Fig. 19a)*, YO and pull up a loop, (YO and draw through 2 loops on hook) twice, YO twice, skip next 3 dc, insert hook from **front** to **back** in center of next Split tr *(Fig. 19b)*, YO and pull up a loop, (YO and draw through 2 loops on hook) twice, YO and draw through all 3 loops on hook.

Fig. 19a

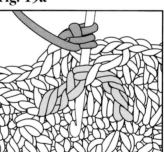

Fig.19b

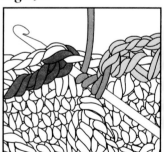

POPCORN

Work specified number of dc in stitch or space indicated, drop loop from hook, insert hook in first dc of dc group, hook dropped loop and draw through *(Fig. 20)*.

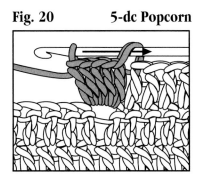

Fig. 20   **5-dc Popcorn**

PUFF STITCH

★ YO, insert hook in stitch indicated, YO and pull up a loop even with loop on hook; repeat from ★ as many times as specified, YO and draw through all loops on hook *(Fig. 21)*.

Fig. 21

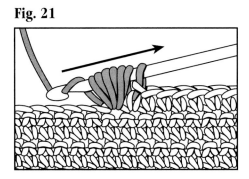

LONG STITCH

Work single crochet (sc), half double crochet (hdc), or double crochet (dc), inserting hook in stitch or space indicated in instructions *(Fig. 22)* and pulling up a loop even with loop on hook; complete stitch.

Fig. 22

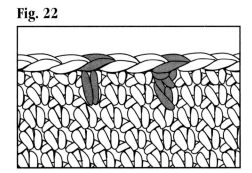

REVERSE SINGLE CROCHET
(abbreviated reverse sc)

Working from **left** to **right**, insert hook in st to right of hook *(Fig. 23a)*, YO and draw through, under, and to left of loop on hook (2 loops on hook) *(Fig. 23b)*, YO and draw through both loops on hook *(Fig. 23c)* (reverse sc made, *Fig. 23d)*.

Fig. 23a

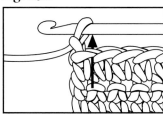

Fig. 23b

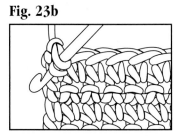

Fig. 23c

Fig. 23d

REVERSE HALF DOUBLE CROCHET
(abbreviated reverse hdc)

Working from **left** to **right**, YO, insert hook in sc indicated to right of hook *(Fig. 24a)*, YO and draw through, under, and to left of loops on hook (3 loops on hook) *(Fig. 24b)*, YO and draw through all 3 loops on hook *(Fig. 24c)* (reverse hdc made, *Fig. 24d)*.

Fig. 24a

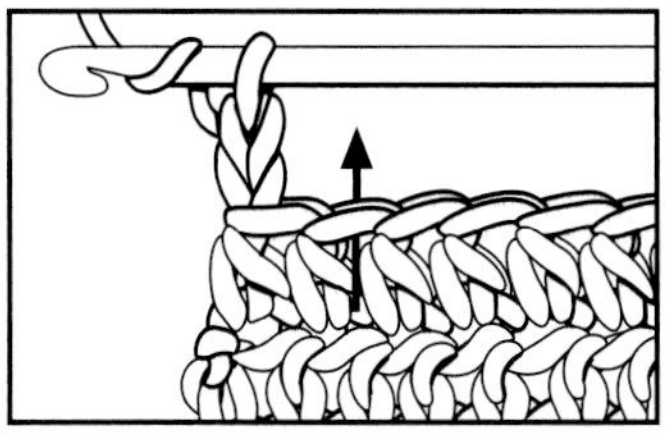

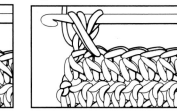

Fig. 24b

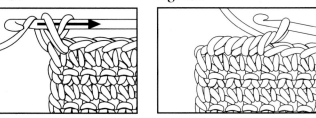

Fig. 24c

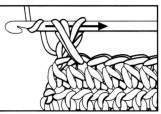

Fig. 24d

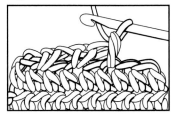

141

STITCHING TIPS

JOINING WITH SC

When instructed to join with sc, begin with a slip knot on hook. Insert hook in stitch or space indicated, YO and pull up a loop, YO and draw through both loops on hook.

BACK OR FRONT LOOP ONLY

Work only in loop(s) indicated by arrow *(Fig. 25)*.

Fig. 25

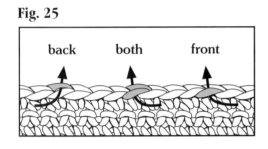

FREE LOOPS

After working in Back or Front Loops Only on a row or round, there will be a ridge of unused loops. These are called the free loops. Later, when instructed to work in the free loops of the same row or round, work in these loops *(Fig. 26a)*. When instructed to work in a free loop of a beginning chain, work in loop indicated by arrow *(Fig. 26b)*.

Fig. 26a

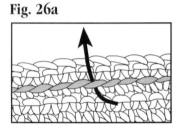

Fig. 26b

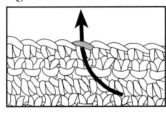

CHANGING COLORS

Work the last stitch to within one step of completion, hook new yarn *(Fig. 27a)* and draw through loops on hook. Cut old yarn and work over both ends unless otherwise specified.
When working in rounds or changing colors with a slip st, drop old yarn; using new yarn, join with slip stitch to first stitch *(Fig. 27b)*.

Fig. 27a

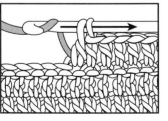

Fig. 27b

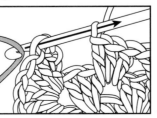

WORKING IN SPACE BEFORE STITCH

When instructed to work in space **before** a stitch or in spaces **between** stitches, insert hook in space indicated by arrow *(Fig. 28)*.

Fig. 28

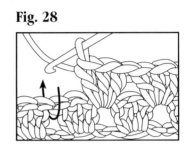

NO-SEW JOINING

Hold Squares, Motifs, or Strips with **wrong** sides together. Slip st or sc into sp as indicated *(Fig. 29)*.

Fig. 29

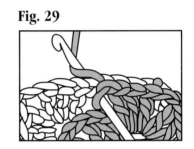

WEAVING IN YARN ENDS

Good finishing techniques make a big difference in the quality of any crocheted piece. Make a habit of weaving in loose ends as you work. **Never** tie a knot in your yarn; a knot may poke through to the right side and will sometimes come untied and unravel. Weaving in the ends gives a much better result. Thread a yarn needle with the yarn end. With **wrong** side facing, weave the needle through several stitches, then reverse the direction and weave it back through several more stitches. When the end is secure, clip the yarn close to your work.
You may also hide your ends as you work by crocheting over them for several inches to secure, then weave in opposite direction; clip the remaining lengths off close to your work. Always check your work to be sure the yarn ends do not show on the right side.

FINISHING

WHIPSTITCH

With **wrong** sides together and beginning in corner stitch, sew through both pieces once to secure the beginning of the seam, leaving an ample yarn end to weave in later. Insert needle from **front** to **back** through **inside** loops of **each** piece *(Fig. 30a)* or through **both** loops *(Fig. 30b)*. Bring needle around and insert it from **front** to **back** through the next loops of **both** pieces. Continue in this manner across to corner, keeping the sewing yarn fairly loose.

Fig. 30a   Fig. 30b

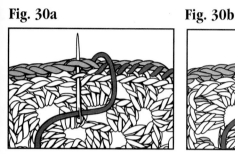

FRINGE

Cut a piece of cardboard 8" wide and ½" longer than desired fringe. Wind the yarn **loosely** and **evenly** around the length of the cardboard until the card is filled, then cut across one end; repeat as needed. Align the number of strands desired and fold in half.

With **wrong** side facing and using a crochet hook, draw the folded end up through a stitch, row, or loop, and pull the loose ends through the folded end *(Figs. 31a & b)*; draw the knot up **tightly** *(Figs. 31c & d)*. Repeat, spacing as specified. Lay flat on a hard surface and trim the ends.

Fig. 31a   Fig. 31b

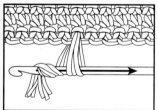
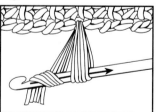

Fig. 31c   Fig. 31d

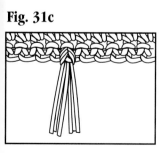
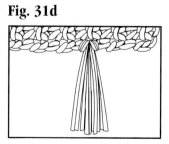

WASHING AND BLOCKING

Before washing or blocking your afghan, check the yarn label for any special instructions. Many acrylics and some blends have special handling instructions and may be damaged during washing and/or blocking.

Many fibers require hand washing, carefully launder your afghan using a mild soap or detergent. Rinse it without wringing or twisting. Remove any excess moisture by rolling it in a succession of dry towels. If you prefer, you may put it in the final spin cycle of your washer — but, do **not** use water. Lay the afghan on a flat surface covered with towels out of direct sunlight. Gently smooth and pat Afghan to the finished size as indicated in the individual instructions. Pin in place using stainless steel pins, when the Afghan is completely dry, it is blocked.

Steaming is an excellent method of blocking afghans, especially those made with wool or wool blends. Turn the afghan to the **wrong** side. Using stainless steel pins, pin afghan on a board covered with towels to the finished size as indicated in the individual instructions. Hold a steam iron or steamer just above the afghan and steam it thoroughly. Never let the weight of the iron touch your item because it will flatten the stitches. Leave the afghan pinned until it is completely dry.

credits

To Magna IV Color Imaging of Little Rock, Arkansas, we say thank you for the superb color reproduction and excellent pre-press preparation.

We want to especially thank photographers Ken West, Larry Pennington, Mark Mathews, and Karen Shirey of Peerless Photography, Little Rock, Arkansas, and Jerry R. Davis of Jerry Davis Photography, Little Rock, Arkansas, for their time, patience, and excellent work.

We would like to extend a special word of thanks to the talented designers who created the lovely projects in this book:

Eleanor Albano: *Casual Comfort*, page 10; *Climbing Roses*, page 28; *Emerald Isle Medley*, page 36; and *Christmas Dazzle*, page 128

Alexander-Stratton: *Victorian Lace*, page 18; *Liberty*, page 80; and *Western Ambiance*, page 100

Jennie Black: *Romantic Diamonds*, page 44

Rose Marie Brooks: *Rock-A-Bye Plaid*, page 34

Nair Carswell: *Freedom Day*, page 92; *Country Pleasures*, page 98; and *Quiet Moments*, page 120

Anne Halliday: *Delightful Medley*, page 8; *Nostalgic Ripple*, page 12; *Simply Kitty*, page 14; *Sweetheart Blanket*, page 20; *Curly Cutie*, page 42; *Tranquil Granny*, page 56; *"Purr-fection!"* page 58; *Cheery Garden*, page 82; *Soothing Waves*, page 90; *Cozy Ripple*, page 94; *Fruited Plains*, page 96; *Tumbleweed*, page 122; and *Snowflakes*, page 132

Jan Hatfield: *Garden Stroll*, page 54

Lucia Karge: *Fit for a King*, page 130

Terry Kimbrough: *Heartwarming Fans*, page 24; *Baby's Circle of Love*, page 32; *Spring Pansies*, page 46; and *Circle of Roses*, page 72

Ann Kirtley: *Absolutely Gorgeous*, page 70, and *Grandeur*, page 102

Jennine Korejko: *Lacy Charm*, page 30

Patricia Kristofferson: *Restful Wrap*, page 68, and *Summer Sherbet*, page 84

Melissa Leapman: *Natural Stripes*, page 88

Carole Prior: *Buffalo Check*, page 6; *Granny's Lilacs*, page 38; *Rainbow Ripple*, page 40; *Summer Symphony*, page 66; *Ebb and Flow*, page 78; *Bricks of Color*, page 106; *Brilliant Ripples*, page 110; and *Autumn Splendor*, page 118

Mary Ann Sipes: *Regal Tones*, page 108, and *Yuletide Blocks*, page 126

Martha Brooks Stein: *Signs of Fall*, page 112

Gail Tanquary: *Cupid's Dream*, page 22, and *Angels in the Clouds*, page 48

Carole Rutter Tippett: *Spiderweb*, page 116